The 'True' Family Values Restored

The Torah fulfilled
The 'Tree of Life' restored
Integrating the universal principles for
psychological/social & spiritual
health

The Last Spiritual Samurai

"For God, to be a man, he must despair."

Albert Camus

...now ALL the children say... 'we don't
need another hero.'

"God's truth is sent to earth as a revelation given through certain providential figures. God's truth is the absolute truth, which is an almighty key capable of solving any problem, no matter how difficult it may be... When this truth is applied to society, social problems can be settled, & when this truth is applied to the world, world problems can be realistically solved... This is a new view of life, a new view of the world, a new view of the universe, & a new view of the providence of history that has never before existed. It is also a principle of integration that can encompass the whole into one unity, while at the same time preserving the individual characteristics of all religious doctrines & philosophies." Rev. Sun Myung Moon

"One can regard the history of the human species, in the large, as the realization of a hidden plan of nature to bring about an internally, & for this purpose, also an externally perfect national constitution, as the sole state in which all of humanity's natural capacity can be developed." Immanuel Kant

"Take responsibility for the most difficult problem in your nation. Take responsibility for the most difficult problem of your church. Take responsibility for the most difficult problem of the world." Rev Sun Myung Moon

Intro... For our 1ˢᵗ Consideration

Declaration: The era of The True Family Values & The Tree of Life Restored...The threshold of 'Hope' substantially offered, gratitude our global behavioral response

Standing proposition: God is not, nor ever was, the issue before us...

The challenge remaining... a reality check in our mirrors

Reintroducing ourselves: The first '2' that climbed Mt Everest

Formal Introduction

"Houston, we have a problem": Global family social protests seek our universal conscience & heart & Jewish history answers

Chapter 1- Listening as our 1st humility & the 'Zen' of freedom: The witness & wisdom of the cosmos vs human truth & knowledge

Chapter 2- Defining a rationale for human nature: Honoring the universal significance of relationships

Chapter 3- Establishing a human vocabulary: building bridges of 'heart' meaning to community & relational maintenance

Chapter 4- The 3 Great Human Virtues: The universal global lineage in the search for human friendly 'values' as principles for living

Declaration: The era of The True Family Values & The Tree of Life Restored... The threshold of 'Hope' substantially offered, gratitude our global behavioral response

"God's truth is sent to earth as a revelation given through certain providential figures. God's truth is the absolute truth, which is an almighty key capable of solving any problem, no matter how difficult it may be... When this truth is applied to society, social problems can be settled, & when this truth is applied to the world, world problems can be realistically solved... This is a new view of life, a new view of the world, a new view of the universe, & a new view of the providence of history that has never before existed. It is also a principle of integration that can encompass the whole into one unity, while at the same time preserving the individual characteristics of all

8

religious doctrines & philosophies." Rev. Sun
Myung Moon

"The whole of the Torah is for the purpose of
promoting peace." Judaism, Talmud, Gittin 59b

"Inter-religious reconciliation and cooperation is an
essential condition for world peace. I have campaigned
tirelessly for interreligious harmony and dialogue... Its
(religion's) first requirement is that the religious people
sacrifice themselves, harmonize and cooperate with other
religions. With this they become capable of advising the
political leaders...

Therefore, religious leaders and believers should be the
guides who lead people to peace. If religions only
emphasize narrow-minded denominationalism and fail to
teach true love for God and the universe, we will never
free humankind from the horrors of war. In the face of this
global crisis, religious leaders have to practice true love,
humbly following God's Will, walking hand in hand
beyond the boundaries of their own religion.

The inner power of religion touches our hearts and can
recreate us as people of peace. It can cultivate our ability

to practice self-control from within. It can overcome historical hatreds and resentments among us. This is the root from which arises true peace & stability

If religions demonstrate love for each other, cooperate with each other, and serve each other, putting the higher ideal of peace ahead of particular doctrines, rituals and cultural backgrounds, the world will change dramatically. Beyond National Self-Interest. Rev. Sun Myung Moon

"Moon's legacy, like that of Jesus, is simple... 8 words form the whole of their theology... 'Become love, forgiving, repenting... & become true parents.'" The Last Spiritual Samurai

It is said in the Torah that Jew will be reconciled with God ONLY when Jews love all other Jews.

There is no greater wisdom offered in the Torah. There is no greater wisdom offered in ANY sacred book, by any great teacher. It is the wisdom of Jewish history, it is the wisdom of 'human' history, OUR history, brought to life in rhetoric, in words that ANY person can digest.

Love your neighbor… this reconciliation the key to liberating our own relationship with God. Or the cosmos.

Yes, hidden right within our sight, in those very words, are such words of wisdom, words for all humanity, be they Jew or not, religious or not, that there is cause for universal hope & celebration.

The cause for celebration?

The values offering such inspiration? That we honor others as not only 'worthy' of our effort to love, we must also surrender to allowing them to love us, in equal measure in heart & behavior. This union the foundation for God to 'appear' between us & 'in' us.

'In' us in the sense of occupying the same 'heart' towards all relationships, expressing the depth of heart we associate with the most loving parents, in their cognitive & rational commitment, to care that much & to that degree of sustained quality.

Why to celebrate? There is everything needed that is needed, all within the grasp & such common moral meaning, as to speak to any human, any parent, any family… any nation. It is our capacity.

The hope revealed?

As we master the values needed to begin the true rebirth of the human species, we may pioneer new paths, that while difficult for us, will only offer those who follow a clearer, more simple learning process.

As we master the values needed to truly care, to master the social skills they naturally reveal, we will become a living proof as to what is possible. The more unlikely you imagine yourself an inspiration to others, the more conscientiously we may also come to invest ourselves in the effort 'to be ourselves', as our new freedom will reveal is possible.

The result? A living witness, humble to the effect, living to honor, living to co-create. Living… to be human.

A joyful offering onto the lord…

This is not so profound, for, you see, to be a 'Jew' also means 'to be human.' Human in that purely human way, meaningful to human experience, potential & need. To be truly 'Jewish' does not actually require one be Jewish, in the religious sense, or even hold any belief in God or gods…

The 'wisdom' of 'being' Jewish is in the nature of the potential for relationships that is nurtured & natured as natural, for each & every individual, & thus natural for & as family. As family, as nation.

For as the wisdom of the Talmud offered, the Torah serves humanity as a means to encourage & move humanity towards the values that can, & will, secure peace, as an interpersonal social & political reality!

When properly interpreted, Jewish history reveals the exact same pattern of socialization we universally recognize as the process EVERY family instigates & experiences in the socialization of our children, this to a future of sustained & inevitable relationships. Jewish history now reveals itself as the Philosopher's Stone sought throughout western history.

Where every major & minor 'teacher' on moral reflection sought the exact same conclusions & recognized the same values, however rhetorically expressed, Jewish history seems to have marshalled all the critical factors into one historical developmental period, lasting millennia, but naturally divided into its native elements & corresponding time periods of integration & mastery.

Elements native to every family, every social process of martialing the values to create a sustainable community, for whatever defined purposes.

God promised Abraham a future… a future not defined, nor limited. Yet, when this relationship was initiated, human history, specifically in this case, Jewish history, by God's design or by some natural evolutionary impulse, history began a journey only now cognitively grasped, rationally interpreted & openly revealed.

Today, just as when the Jews stood before its first true son, we have the opportunity to make a revolutionary decision & first step. We can assume a degree of morally significant opportunity that has not existed for over 2000 years.

In doing so, in assuming responsibility for what was revealed so long ago, that humanity needs & is critical not only to our hopes for conflict management & for prosperity as a species, it is the needed key to prevent our extinction, a very real possibility, long term or in the short.

What Rev. Martin Luther King, Jr. imagined was the solution to the salvation of a civilization, is no less so for the individual, the society of any nation as well as for any global community. To remind us… "There is still a voice crying out in terms that echo across the generations, saying; Love your enemies, bless them that curse you, pray for them that despitefully use you, that you may be the children of your Father which is in heaven. This love might well be the salvation of our civilization."

Revelatory research into Jewish history now reveals what 'Pauline' Christianity hid from us; the true values that Jesus both articulated defined the true child of God, hence the truly human, but in doing so, hid the very values needed by ALL humanity, & specifically, our families, as the ONLY means to not only create sustainable true love families, but in doing so, introduces the truly human to the greater 'society' beyond the family.

But a societal member capable of such a quality of sustained, morally significant integration, as to be a natural asset to any community so vested in.

This accomplished through the socialization of The True Family Values, the restored rational understanding of human potential, the nature of God, if God exists, revealed in human terms, digestible to human rationality, integration & incorporation.

The path to the Tree of Life is revealed in Jewish history, as a lesson to all humanity, their siblings yet to be recognized, & if recognized in the heart, then embraced as family.

With the revelation of the REAL nature of the sociological development that was Jewish history, humanity is liberated to reconsider itself in a global, familial context, a species needing moral direction, to survive itself, that the cosmos might survive humanity.

Jewish history revealed is the Philosopher's Stone, but it requires that EVERY person engages the potential revealed, to reap its implied & specific benefits. Benefits that strangely ONLY emerge in the context & ecosystem that honors the value of EVERY individual as sacred, but celebrated in a sustained community of equally imagined & embraced individuals; a community of such individuals.

This then, naturally mind you, restoring 'beloved community' back to human experience.

Where Christians imagined a world where Jew does not REALLY matter anymore, we now discover that without the history of Israel to guide us, inspire us & judge us, we will flounder forever, lost to ourselves.

Now, the Jewish people themselves face the same judgement the rest of us must suffer, to be free, to rediscover our own true potential for being fully human. But this is a judgement we must share, must engage with one another. We must discover the REAL meaning of family, as a species or as a creation.

The ONLY perfect image of myself, is when I engage a perfect reflection of the same values, even if uniquely packaged & expressed. THAT is the joy of discovery. That I could be so cool, in so many other forms. For what I now observe are all the wonderful varieties of my 2nd selves that were always there, but that I had not yet recognized as such, & honored as such.

Jesus, the 1st truly human son of Israel, realized the standard of interpersonal moral values that logic would dictate as a conclusion to the nature & content of Jewish history, & as offering natural evidence of a sociological phenomena of moral evolution. This conclusion that Jesus reached became a living statement then of both personal & public purpose, both in its living content he offered as a personal witness, but also in the nature of the 'hope' he then sought to impart to his 'natural,' even if an artificially created, family. God the external agent, 'forcing' a community to emerge, singularly both responsive to & responsible to God. This to be a morally indicated responsibility. This responsibility now fulfilled in the 'way of being' Jewish history would indicate God sought, that of filial children, honoring their 'parent' in the mimicry of values offered, not to God, but to one another, of the value they held for the parent.

Hence, Jesus offered two simultaneous hopes.

The hope of a conclusion of a quality of history that would mark a new direction for humanity, based upon a re-birth of the idea of a morally significant social responsibility to one another, plus recognizing & acting upon opportunity & thus employing the needed exercise of personal freedom & its native disciplines. A new future for humanity, ONLY realized in the quality of sustainable relationships now sought to be the norm.

But also a hope that speaks to each of us, in our own heart of hearts. The belief that even 'we' have an unrealized potential, both in the giving & in the receiving. A deeply held & profound notion that we matter...

A hope that we can 'reveal the true children' of our heavenly father, in the quality of sustainable commitment we can make, to ourselves, representing our commitment then also to all others, offered under all the conditions of social challenge humanity produces. A hope that we, too, can 'be perfect' as our parent in heaven.

A hope Jesus offered that we may feel the need to challenge, because he was the ONLY living witness to its human potential, as a realizable individual & social reality. (But a hope that once understood, in the heart, becomes a greater drug than any natural or human created drug…)

In the process of engaging the 'perfect' Jesus, we may imagine him a god… seemingly then beyond the pale. Someone to admire, maybe even express an emotionally defined filial piety towards… But, where does that leave us? Do we have any greater 'obligation'?

Two factors support his position as socially realizable not only for us, but also as authentic to its content as a global human living potential. Most important to note is the singularity of the message, a message he defended even with his life. The continuity of effort in this regard, the singularity of focus of rhetoric, the singularity of purpose, to defend a social moral inevitability of cosmic proportions, was evident in the witness offered by disciples. Second, & critical to our integrity as humans, supposedly mature, is that the essence of his criticism, that humanity is not really serious about its moral commitments, was true & is at the heart of not only the core unmet problem, but the challenge life itself poses to us.

Jewish history offers a 'God' whose attendance is everything ANY truly loving parent would do, even with deviant & willfully harmful children.

God offered the first evidence of the nature of the commitment made. It was to be the nature of the relationship to be shared. A God caring about & for humanity, so humanity, in the image of God, as a reflection of God, as a measure of the love of a child for its parent, would then mimic that behavior, coming to understand its value, in the shared meaning created as a sustained statement of relationship… & thus, community, beloved community.

In understanding the nature of & the continuity of both the development of Jewish history & its natural & social meanings, we discover all the forms of love life demands of humanity, to be the true children of God… or the cosmos.

Natively structured to reflect both human experience & core needs, both as a moral & meaning seeking creature, but also to survive much less prosper, the values revealed in Jewish history, whither the source, the values defined by that history are the key to our needs.

Jewish history reveals the values EVERY parent needs to master, to offer to their own children the quality of experiences to truly liberate them in their own self creation as patriot/citizens.

These values require first the disciplined quality of commitment to oneself that is ultimately self-defining.

Those who have achieved greatness in some way, that required the measured giving of oneself totally to one's purpose, they would understand the heart that Jesus offered was both natural to being a child of God... but also to be as an aid to God, to speak for God, as Jesus was.

Yet, rather than to embellish oneself for success in the world, Jesus offered that 'to be Jewish' was to be a true child of God, but now fully living that life, as a disciplined measure of heart, the will to care the key to all behavior.

Jewish history & its prophets & teachers, like all the moral teachers of history, knew of 'the will to care' & its significance to the quality of life we endure... or share. All history speaks to commitments to care, to offering, to repentance as life celebration, to forgiveness as the living evidence of God's living presence among humanity.

Now, in the clarity of the revelation that is history, we discover the Torah fulfilled. We discover the 'way of peace' for ALL humanity revealed for all to gather for themselves.

FOR THE VALUES REVEALED ARE NOT RELIGIOUS VALUES, EVEN IF THEY REFLECT THE VALUES WE UNDERSTAND INFORM THE HEART OF GOD & THE SOCIAL ACTIONS TAKEN BY GOD.

The values revealed by history, from God or the product of human social evolution, their content is human in its potential both for application & sufficient meaning as to offer HEALING.

Humanity needs two kinds of healing.

The first being the healing that comes with loving offering.

The second healing comes with in receiving love offerings.

Both healings fortunately are very effectively realized in relationships of conflict & harm. In the experience of deviance, as the perpetrator or the victim, love takes its own form, its own contextual content. That is the exercise of freedom, revealed as wisdom.

When cognitively recognizable as a codified & structured form of morally significant interpersonal values, natural to both human experience & as a set of needed social skills as parents, The True Family Values emerge as the ONLY possible rationale & potential moral paradigm to offer not just hope to humanity, but the way forward.

2000 years after Jesus, a strange little Korean man burst upon the American, & then, global political & religious scene, arguing for a revival of Christianity.

But, strangely, his Jesus & his Christianity were not recognizable to American white Christians, or their global counterpart.

Moon's Jesus was, when closely examined & understood, which it is not to this day, even by its own members, Moon's Jesus was the same Jesus that Jewish history now defends as a true son of Israel, &, as a global, yet unrecognized avatar for humanity.

Both also offered their lives to the exact same message, when understood contextually, as a historical drama of global significance.

When formed as a complete idea/paradigm, God's actions, in human translation & offered response, reveal The True Family Values. These are the Keys to the Kingdom promised Christians. They are the Philosopher's Stone for ALL humanity to engage & employ. The True Family Values are the key to The Tree of Life.

With their mastery, such informed relationships have an opportunity of such socially significant moral realization as is beyond our current conflict dominated imaginations to yet comprehend.

Two factors will confuse & discourage us.

First, we have prioritized our emotional identities such that they actually act as a greater moral authority than we even allow God... or our conscience. This, coupled with a 'will to care' that is at least retarded, if not actually crippled, we are lost children, but adults, who do adult damage & harm.

Acting with the 'will to care' & reprioritizing our emotional priorities & values restructured to embrace & employ The True Family Values, one may discover one is increasingly in conflict with one's social environment.

Then our commitment 'to will to care' will be challenged on its first leg of needed discipline. The effort will be slow, with more failures than successes. But each recognized failure is progress. We now 'see' where once we were blind.

In this, we have stepped out of the grave of history.

We become hope.

The vision of self never before fully imagined. Fully fleshed out.

Jesus comes to life.

God is recognized.

Moon is now family.

So is my enemy.

This is our gratitude.

Consider: God is not the issue before us... nor ever was. We, as the Mud Nation, are. We, as we stand together, or alone, we are the issue. Today, we can take on that issue...

"God's repentance, at the fall of humanity, led to the quality of forgiveness we now embrace in Jesus & Moon, as God's children. That we then 'pay forward' as our gratitude, offered to others, in our social behavior. The True Family Values are the revelation of ALL God's forms of loving humanity. Forms now native to human consumption & creation, in the experiences we create for ourselves, as the people of the word seeking to be the children of God."

"You deplore the demonstrations that are presently taking place... But I am sorry that your statement did not express a similar concern for the conditions that brought the demonstrations into being." Rev. Martin Luther King, Jr.

"But communists, fascists, terrorists of all ilk, domestic & foreign, Nazi's & American racist white nationalists, all worship the same god... choose who & what you hate, then proceed to destroy what you hate, by any means possible. Hence, never admitting that while the opposite side is the enemy, as communist encounters white nationalist, they agree on one thing... the tools to persuade, that begin with hateful rhetoric & end with bullets." The Last Spiritual Samurai

"All interpretation of meaning, like all scientific observation, strives for clarity & verifiable accuracy of insight & comprehension. The basis for certainty in understanding can either be rational, which can be further subdivided into logical & mathematical, or it can be of an emotionally empathic & artistically appreciative quality... The highest degree of rational understanding is attained in cases involving the meanings of logically or mathematically related propositions; their meaning may be immediately & unambiguously intelligible." Max Weber

"My people go into exile for want of knowledge." Isaiah 5:13

"Let us not wallow in the valley of despair, I say to you today, my friends.

And so even though we face the difficulties of today and tomorrow, I still have a dream. It is a dream deeply rooted in the American dream.

I have a dream that one day this nation will rise up and live out the true meaning of its creed: "We hold these truths to be self-evident, that all men are created equal."
I have a dream that one day on the red hills of Georgia, the sons of former slaves and the sons of former slave owners will be able to sit down together at the table of brotherhood.

I have a dream that one day even the state of Mississippi, a state sweltering with the heat of injustice, sweltering with the heat of oppression, will be transformed into an oasis of freedom and justice.

I have a dream that my four little children will one day live in a nation where they will not be judged by the color of their skin but by the content of their character. I have a *dream* today!" Rev. Martin Luther King, Jr

"This is supposed to be a Christian nation, but tremendous damage has been done to the world... the good Christian moral & cultural tradition is gone... The Protestant & Catholic culture will never do for the future..." Rev. Sun Myung Moon

"The purpose of this essay is once again to face the reality of the present, which is logical crime, & to examine meticulously the arguments by which it is justified; it is an attempt to understand the times in which we live." Albert Camus

"The state of peace must therefore be *established*, for the suspension of hostilities does not provide the security of peace, & unless this security is pledged by one neighbor to another (which can happen only in a state of *lawfulness*), the latter, from whom security has been requested, can treat the former as enemy." Emmanuel Kant

I was almost 72 years old before I realized… & remembered, that my 1st memory of a birthday or any Christmas occurred when I was 8 years old. There were no Christmas' before that. There was NEVER a birthday 'party'. Actually, this was the first period in my life when I now was supposed to also have a father. Whatever that was. Given what 'mother' meant… & didn't.

The toys we had until then fit a shoe box… half full. Yet, for me, for my brother, it was normal. It was life. There was no complaint to be made, much less any person to complain to.

This was my world. My half brother shared it with me. But we did not share our worlds.

You were not part of our world. It was its own universe.

Lest we get off on the wrong foot… we are here to address the human condition, created by humans, sustained by humans… all as a matter of human choice. All the result of the use of our much touted & paraded 'free will.'

We seek to confront the reasons for our suffering, & what our options are, & how they match our needs. What gaps are then left that need be identified & responded to?

Yet, today, we must also categorically state that EVERYTHING IMPORTANT to human potential, human freedom, human meaning, life, health & prosperity, are ALL WITHIN THE REIGN & RIGHTS OF HUMANITY TO REPAIR, RESTORE & RE-FOCUS.

Today, when our values are reoriented to the nature of life itself, we discover the greater meaning & value of freedom. We discover the vision of a quality of individuality never before imagined. We 'see' ourselves through a different lens, a lens that offers more than hope.

Hence, our efforts here are for our benefit, as individuals, & as evolving, morally significant groups. Here stressing ONLY our opportunities, freedom, needs, critical values & social structures inherent to what it must come to mean, "to be human," a human, being.

Whether God exists or not, the challenge was & is the same… WHAT WILL WE, HUMANITY, DO, AS OUR PART… WHAT WILL WE DECIDE IS ULTIMATELY IMPORTANT TO US, EACH OF US, INDIVIDUALLY & AS A SPECIES, & THEN ACT AS TO FULLY & PROPERLY REPRESENT OURSELVES TO THE COSMOS… AS A SPECIES 'WORTHY' TO EXIST AMONG THE COSMOS?

Today, we re-examine ourselves, to liberate ourselves to a degree of freedom, autonomy & moral & psychological health we only imagined was possible.

Today, we leave God, gods & demons behind.

Today… we move to reclaim our humanity.

Today, we define what it means 'to be human' that we might 'be human'.

Today, we re-examine history, to discover our common & universal heritage that we share with all others, religiously motivated or of a secular nature.

The Mud Nation is my reference to those of us who accept that our bodies, if not our natures, arose out of the primordial matter of Mother Earth & the cosmos. That is, earth & water, together forming the 'mud' that is our bodies. Created here, refined here, our bodies stand as the ultimate witness as to the success of the cosmos as a creative force for life, creating a physical form that not only witnesses to the significance of relationships, but in the nature of its success, argues there is a 'morality' that 'governs' all such success.

While all humanity shares in this inheritance, the minute they are born, it is a distinction that comes with a burden. How shall we imagine ourselves; how shall we therefore imagine each other? What shall that then dictate as 'wisdom' for human choice? What are the moral implications of relationship that must guide our defining of our humanity?

What we do has significance. Individually & collectively. To ourselves & to the environment we are a part of. Thus, we matter, each & everyone, even if the value others place on us does not share in a celebration of that fact. But we do matter, & the earth, in its own form of ultimate wisdom, has provided us the tools to make an evolutionary jump in the 'nature' that shall be known as human. To make a break with that history. Offering us a new idea of what needs constitute our 'instinct,' that defines our humanity, as individuals & as a species.

Mud Nation then is that portion of the populace who have come to terms with that realization, have accepted it & thus, as inheritors of a 'creation' not of our own creation, we seek to act as conscious, cognitively invested, conscientious actors in a universe in which life is a rarity, sacred in that rarity & not a norm.

In this creative genius that the cosmos offers in the witness of our own bodies, we are also taught about the 'mechanical form of love' that argues a natural morality is inherent to the success of life, to exist, much less prosper. Thus, we recognize that there is a moral dimension to being human, to honor that which we did not create, but continues to support us with every bit of its 'own being.'

Yet, if life offers there is a 'moral' nature to the cosmos, then what is our opportunity? To explore its potential for human employment & value? Is there a moral imperative for the human species? If so, how will we recognize it?

The answer is simple, really. Human reason, properly motivated & sincerely engaged, will offer to us what we might need to begin a proper analysis of the ultimate opportunity for the human species. My hope, is that with time, humanity will allocate the resources needed to begin a true journey into a long-range view needed for a proper human social evolution & will make a corresponding readjustment in the priorities that define the values we use to inform our behaviors. That we begin to seek to define the values that will inform our expectations of the human creature, as a morally accountable & cognitively enabled reflective creature.

This is where our concern with Jesus comes in & the greatest challenge emerges for non-Christians & especially those of us who are atheists who care about a proper order for humanity.

My research, inspiration, reflection & meditation has revealed some historical anomalies that are significant to the human cause & our morally developing history. Namely, that a proper study of Jewish history reveals a pattern that is sociologically significant not only to religious people, specifically the brother/sister of Judaic/Christianity, but whose synergistic pattern linking 4000 years of history has an ultimate & unavoidable bearing on what it means 'to be human.'

Our job, as intellectually honorable people, is to seek what 'wisdom' this 'revelation' may offer to aid our need for defining a human nature. Hence, if history reveals a timeless, sociologically significant pattern of development, then the 'source' of that movement in history, as a religious source or secular, is not as important immediately as seeking what it may mean for us as a species.

This insight offers that human history is not just the history of our predatory behavior towards each other & the earth, but that history is also progressive, proactive, synergistic & evolutionary in its response to human opportunity & moral need & ultimately, in its message, cumulative. The 'end-product' of that human history, Jesus & his misunderstood social significance to all humanity, is what is of interest to us here, as morally accountable individuals & communities. That, & Moon as a final commentary on that message & mission.

31

'Did' Jesus offer insights to what it means 'to be human' that needs to be extracted from all that he supposedly said & did, that given equal weight, will conclude the social, morally significant evolutionary development that was Jewish history? Is the pathway to 'The Tree of Life' now unhindered, but for the right heart & corresponding effort?

I assert that those who were part of this 'experiment' in 'social engineering,' in Israel's history, did not cognitively grasp the process they were a part of, but that we today, can celebrate that history & the contribution it makes to developing a truly moral human nature; that eventually will define our whole species, not merely as a matter of survival, nor just for the sake of some idealized prosperity.

Hence, we need to resurrect that history, those contributing individuals & decipher the mystery that reveals that somehow, 'divinely driven' or the result of purely sociologically significant social forces, history reveals a hope long unrecognized, but now available to us as a cognitively accessible potential.

What I have discovered, is that Jesus, as a human, is even more relevant to the human cause than we could have imagined, even to those of us who are rationally realized atheists. This reality emerging out of a history we never fully understood. Today, that history reveals a new view of history, of humanity itself... & the future & the way forward.

In this, we discover a true Jewish son, Jesus, calls to us, even more profoundly than to those of 'the faith,' because to truly understand Jesus, we must view history as not ending in some divine comedy. A divine comedy in which humanity is divided into the 'deserving', the 'entitled' & 'chosen', & then, the damned, but rather, a history in which Jesus was responding directly to the needs of humanity, in that human history & as a result of that human history.

IOW's, Jesus offered human solutions to human problems, meant to be applied in the here & now, as humans, as a corrective to human history, religious or otherwise. Non-religious, purely human solutions, arising from the values that we use to inform our motives & behaviors. We will discover just how much Jesus did care about humanity & the legacy he leaves the atheist no less than any person who professes the 'faith to move mountains.'

Today, we are freed to become human...

The True Family Values, the encapsulation & cognitively recognizable & structured wisdom of Jewish history, will be discovered as not only foundational values needed to parent, but they are also the same values needed to redirect human history, as much for the nation as any individual & their family.

In the end, we, as an atheist, Hindu, Christian, Jew, Muslim & all others, will discover we were never really in competition with each other, rather we sought the same answers; each 'teacher' then sharing what they had discovered & could authenticate in their own lives & living.

Jewish history will need to be understood as to what it was... one effort of humanity, seeking the path to the quality of civility we not only imagined we are entitled to, but are capable of producing, as our true acts of freedom & individuality.

Each teacher in history offering all they had learned, had mastered.

Hence, having the authority to impart to us what parts of the puzzle they could.

But all such individuals in history, Jesus, the Prophet, Buddha, King, Gandhi, Moon, our feminists, our civil rights activists, our environmental champions… all seeking but one solution. The means to change the ways & means of the values that are used to so harm humanity.

Today, we unite as one community.

Today, we seek answers as a community.

The source is less important than the values informing the solutions. It is living solutions we seek, not gods & ideologies.

Those 'living' values lived, will authenticate the authority of their final contributing authors. We honor our teachers when we act as if we are the teachers.

It is then 'we' are called to the plate… what can WE offer?

Maybe more than we ever previously imagined. Maybe freedom is closer than we know, one choice away.

'Judgement Day' & The Challenge Remaining: A reality check in our mirrors

"If you wish to untie a knot, you must first understand how it was tied." Buddhism

"History reveals two qualities of rebels to history. Those that seek to be a benefit to the world, including to their enemy, in their own offering, & those who seek to re-imagine & re-create the world, but without their enemy, as a result of assuming the right to eliminate the enemy. This, rather than to integrate with the enemy, as an act of community creation & social & historical restoration." The Last Spiritual Samurai

"Leadership should not be a question of charisma, how the image affects us as an emotionally compelling component, but rather leadership should be contextually considered as a matter of principles to define motive, to inform & guide behavior. This demanded standard of behavior a sustained state expressed across all social mediums, personal, public & political. Leadership is ultimately about the principles of civility, of parenting &

of social cohesion. Of community, as a morally significant integration of sacred individuals." The Last Spiritual Samurai

"The established religions & their adherents have never realized that man has a central responsibility for turning this evil world around." Rev. Sun Myung Moon

"Religion is no more 'righteous' than the principles that define it & the 'success,' or 'faith,' of its adherents. Religion, as a human enterprise, to serve human interest, should serve humanity in its needs & purposes, not become an object of worship itself. It is people that matter." The Last Spiritual Samurai

"The developed nations of the world should feel that they have been blessed by God for the purpose of helping others. They must be willing to offer themselves for the underdeveloped nations of the world. If the prosperous nations do not think in loftier terms than the desire for profits, their prosperity will slip away in spite of their efforts to retain it." Rev. Sun Myung Moon

"be ye therefore perfect as your parent in heaven..." Jesus

There is a great difference between the results of 'judgement' when received as guilt & accusation & when one receives judgement & it produces shame. A shame, that in its expression, still affirms the heart-held significance of relationship to all affected.

Shame is a rationally engaged, emotionally significant state wherein we assume a responsibility for the informing motives & their environmental impact, that we would now have managed much differently, if possible. In contrast to that past, now, the desire is to 'restore' the relationship(s) affected. Guilt, as a contrasting emotionally significant response, is the emotional content when we receive the same judgment, but the result is fear & the overriding defined need for self-defense. The viewing of all others as in an adversarial role & a 'potential' enemy. It is now 'me' VS them.

Shame, as an expression of 'heart', or our commitment to care, that defines us as human, allows us to entertain a vulnerability & intimacy with others during the process of accountability. Shame allows us to seek the aid of others, aid to restore the damage done, the hearts harmed. Shame allows us to feel others will aid us in our restorative efforts. Shame acts as a binding factor to events otherwise damaged, but now in a receivership of all involved.

Guilt, as an emotional response, in its self-defense, seeks to deny responsibility, in part or in whole. They fear others, they resist them for the fear of payment (an indemnity condition beyond their control or appeal) that will be required, forced & that will deny freedom, hence deny our sense of humanity. As we denied others humanity in the harms created, intended or not.

Today, all humanity faces Judgement Day.

Today, in the global revelation of The True Family Values, Christians can no longer deny their inheritance…nor their inherited responsibility, to both God, & to all the 'other' children of God. Our siblings.

Instead, in the failure of Christians to be instructed in the true & full message of Jesus, as history intended by the nature of its internal development, Christianity became more of a self-interested & self-serving corporation. Thus, more focused on its own agenda, as opposed to that originally defined & defended by Jesus himself. The individual & collective consequence being, today, Christians have not realized the spiritual/psychological maturity that is both the potential of humanity, as individuals & as a species, but also the will of God as expressed in the Holy Bible, containing the sacred scriptures of both Jew & Christian. Problematically, even with the advocacy of Rev. Sun Myung Moon of both Jesus & his true message, Christians again failed to recognize the spirit & message of Jesus in the message of Moon.

Hence, spiritual & a proper psychological growth, critical to the health of humanity as individuals but also as families & nations, as intended by God & history, was thwarted not only at the time of Jesus… it has not been understood or integrated into Christianity to date. Moon's offering was spurned, as a matter of a racist response, but also coupled with an unearned arrogance about Christian's own spiritual status, as Americans, as opposed to a Korean, from Korea.

The commandment demanded by Jesus, that we realize a maturity or spiritual perfection, 'be ye therefore perfect as your 'parent' in heaven,' has been glossed over as NOT emotionally or spiritually compelling. Yet, paradoxically, we discover it is this very misunderstanding that has prevented the message & mission of Jesus to be understood globally, universally, with the effect that the nation that honors itself as 'Christian', is in all actuality, not that at all. Hence, in the failure to understand Jesus, coupled with the failure to recognize the message of Jesus in Moon's words & life effort, then Christians once again, like their Jewish counterparts, were & are now up the proverbial creek.

Rev. Moon's own group has now encountered the same challenge... they do not yet fully grasp the meaning of 'messiah', as for its specific content & relevance, to the human spiritual & psychological condition, as individuals, families & as a species. Hence, the spiritual/psychological maturity demanded by Jesus is somehow lacking, or, when considered, emotionally is too taxing to even consider & therefore, seems insurmountable. Not worth the effort.

The spiritual challenge to such an indicated perfection/maturity actually emerges because WE as yet do NOT understand the true full & ONLY message Jesus & Moon NEEDED to communicate, to fulfill their potential social roles. This as opposed to the message we prefer from them. A message of tolerance & patience, that all is forgiven, rather than the heart of attendance to Jesus & God that would produce the fruits Jesus required we MUST produce. Contrary to popular myth, Jesus' & God's implied love, as forgiveness, is NOT a blank check towards the future... Today, we want to clarify that missing final element that challenges us so, taxes our very heart & willingness to even try to be God's true children.

It is time to order our universes, to master the 'heart of the dragon'... This centers around our assumed & self-created emotional identity, its content & it's effect upon our decisions involving our owned & unowned motives. The natural challenge we have yet to own & meet then revealed in spades, in the noonday sun, in the subsequent behaviors offered to others... via relationships. Relationships, the key to life.

Our emotions & emotional identity are out of order, & this disorder prevents us from recognizing the final steps needed to engage the capacity to be fully human, a true child of God. Mature. The perfect witness to the cosmos' own contribution to life... & ultimately, living free.

Today, as we come to understand the relationship between our emotional identity & our human potential & need, we will also recognize how to order that identity so that it serves the greater purpose... to love & to be loved.

Today, our emotional identity will be placed in its proper order, so that the will of God... & the true potential of humanity, can be understood & acted upon to produce the truly mature, 'the perfect children of God & the Cosmos.'

Children who view others as unique expressions of the same quality of being each seeks for themselves, as they seek to love & to be loved, as a natural statement of being human, of being alive...

Today, we transform, by transcending what was, with the vision of what must be... for us 'to be human.'

That is the remaining challenge: to choose what it shall mean... 'to be human'... being human. This will define the individual no less than the parent... & no less than the true patriot. Or... to the religious, the definition of what it will mean... to be a true child of God.

Or even just a true child of the cosmos... revealing the jewel of creation.

You... me... us.

Re-introducing 'ourselves': The first '2' that climbed Mt. Everest

"All true effort to help begins with self-humiliation: the helper must 1ˢᵗ humble himself under him he would help, & therein must understand that to help does not mean to be sovereign but to be a servant, that to help means to endure for the time being the imputation that one is in the wrong & does not understand what the other understands." Kierkegaard

"Ever since the fall of humanity away from its destiny, Heavenly Parent has sought those who could bear the shame forgiveness exposes, so that Heavenly Parent could then offer the tools needed to reverse & restore history. This was the search for a true heart." The Last Spiritual Samurai

"Paul never met the historical Jesus. Yet, as a result of a religious experience in which he believed he had encountered the crucified & risen Christ, the persecutor of Christians abandoned his former life & carried out his 'call' to preach the 'good news' to the Gentiles... the heart of this 'good news' is 'not' the perpetuation of the teachings of Jesus or of having a 'Christ-like' moral life in the sense of following in the steps of Jesus... rather, the center is the 'Christ-event,' that is, Jesus' death on the cross & his resurrection from the dead." Norman Perrin, Dennis C. Duling

"True leadership establishes the standard... but one we imagine suited to all leaders, hence, all parents, therefore, all our children. Truly loving children mimic the best of the values of their parents. This is no less true for all our spiritual leaders. Such leadership operating as a 2nd tier form of parenting & parental example itself." The Last Spiritual Samurai

(Disclaimer: this manuscript deals with 2 religious figures, who inspired 2 inter-related religious traditions, one held to be the proper 'rebirth' of the other. But, the message of BOTH is for ALL HUMANITY, that has been supported historically by every main thinker, religious figure & good parent. Two carried the flame of human needed 'truth' farther than any of their historical siblings, such as Gandhi, King, Moses, Mohammad, Buddha... THE MESSAGE OF BOTH, SANS THE RELIGION, IS THE SAME...DEMANDING THOSE VALUES & THE CORRESPONDING EFFORT THAT WILL LEAD US TO OUR OWN TRUE UNIQUE POTENTIAL, as individuals & as a collective we imagine is HUMANITY. A potential that EXISTS FOR ALL HUMANITY, BEYOND ANY RELIGIOUS consideration.)

To be reminded, Jesus offered that perfection of heart was not only realizable, but actually required for us to establish the natural relationship to God & each other God imagined.

Was Jesus bull-shitting us when he demanded this? Most today, in Moon's church or Jesus', are in doubt as to the true meaning of those words. I remember reading a comment by a black American leader who wisely, if bluntly, offered the critique of white Americans in their ways of imagining integrating with black America is NOT to share the same quality of blunt 'truth' about life & living that they would NEVER imagine withholding from their own children.

He rightly judged white Americans as thus NOT loving their co-community members. For we were again acting racist, denying others what we would NEVER deny our own.

The comment stopped me immediately in my tracks. It struck a cord… Could this be true? Had I participated in such behavior myself, innocently or not?

But it did one thing for me… I now committed myself to NEVER imagine that anything I would offer my daughter, would not also be equally available to any other person. This to be the substantiation of my desire to love all, equally.

When I discovered that I did not truly grasp the social & political significance of Jesus & his words, I went on a special mission to end this ignorance.

Don't get me wrong, I have since discovered that the state of most of Christianity is actually worse off than I was when I started. This because where I now had a heart of desire for the kind of 'knowledge' that the average person finds 'bothersome' & not emotionally appealing, I also found I was alone, most self-satisfied with their own understanding.

Christians & other 'saved' people thought, & think, they had 'bought' an unconditional ticket to heaven. Little do they understand Jesus. Or God. Thus, even less have true faith. A faith that is uniquely Jewish/human, as ONLY Jesus was. A faith ONLY revealed in behavior, as the witness to the values chosen, & then acted upon. Thus, the heart revealed, the inner sanctum shared as we would in family.

I discovered it was NOT HERE that I would find the social conscience & heart of Americans. THAT designation would be reserved for those whom few thank, & less honor... our social protestors, who defend the human, to be human, by NOT denying human. Our social conscience revealed in our feminists, our social activists of many colors; those confronting racial & civil rights issues, our environmentalists, seeking to save what others would indiscriminately use & use up, destroying what's left behind. As some right of domination & right to subjugation... substantiating THE THEME.

Thanks to the effort of a member of Rev. Moon's theological students, when one individual asked me to review his thesis, his being Japanese, I was confronted by a quote from Moon that actually has initiated a revolution, both in my understanding of Moon, but it also perfectly refocused me on Jesus, his words, & then, the history that led to Jesus & produced the particular cultural form he became, as a messianic figure.

In this quote, Moon made the absolute statement that if we could not love our enemy, even to the enemy of God, then we could neither act as the 'revealed' children of their parent, nor could we then expect to share an eternity with mutuality of full & mature relationship with God.

This seemed a bit beyond the pale of the message trafficked by white Christian America. A big gap exists. Why? That looming question then forced me to re-evaluate Jesus' words, to ascertain whether they were ultimately & 100% in accord with the respective messages offered by Christian leadership.

Especially in a country which exhorts the world as to its being a Christian nation, when such leadership is obviously morally floundering & no longer offering the leadership, vision & moral structure Jesus offered, we are left adrift. It is unfathomable that the average Christian can now imagine to support such values that derail a nation from its own true values, morally & politically, as we have become, & still imagine itself worthy of salvation, worthy of an unconditional forgiveness that demands no 'day of judgement'.

As we look around, our most rational & reasonable brothers & sisters give witness, year in & year out, that humanity is creating a sustained hell, only varying in the creative genius of ways & means to create… & justify hate, as a living human meme. Hence, a sinful world or a world morally insane & psychologically in denial, humanity itself cries for help. Our feminists, our civil rights activists, our environmental defenders, all bleed the heart of humanity, suffered for millennia.

But no relief is offered by Christianity or its leaders. If anything, Christianity now the greatest propagator of ill will & even more evil, as social & political behaviors. Promoting racism, sexism, environmental exploitation.

In contrast, even in the extreme form as Jesus demanded, as our measure of faith, Moon was appearing to offer what might be the ONLY honest & mature means to rectify the hell we had created… & co-create each day.

45

So, in our considerations, where was Moon & Jesus, as spiritual cousins at least, when it came to such absolutes that challenge the way we are, the way we choose to be, the species with no home yet, no way of being that is truly & just 'human'?

In time, after much internal suffering & much external rejection & humiliation, I would be properly rewarded.

This was of particular importance to me, since I had come to accept that Moon himself stood on the foundation Jesus himself had laid, & further, Moon claimed he therefore represented not only Jesus' interest in humanity, Moon was asserting that with him, his message & mission, the whole of the effort of Jesus, was now consummated & complete.

Thus, Moon was ALSO asserting that what was NOT completed with Jesus, was now completed IN Moon.

But, as my research led me farther & farther astray of the initial efforts to reintroduce myself to Jesus, I discovered a pattern of representation of core values that ONLY were defended by Jesus… & then, Moon.

This led me even farther afield. Could what I was beginning to suspect, actually be true?

Had I discovered the 'core' of what not only defined Jesus, but was ONLY shared by Moon, not only as the qualifying standard for personal maturity, as a child of God, but also as a completed human, being human?

Was the messiah actually the 1st true human, being human?

In the early 80's, when I attended university for a couple of years, my focus on speech communication, the #1 most unconsciously used human capacity, I realized the primacy of communication to every aspect of life & living, including our moral & ethical lives.

I came to realize that as a human behavior, we were sorely lacking in any true 'theology' of human-to-human communication. Then, this awareness led me back to the source of all human misery & suffering... relationships & the morally significant interpersonal values that arm & inform them.

With the emerging map of Jesus, Jewish history, & the one original guiding quote of Moon, I was now refocused on the very playing field that defines any messiah... relationships that are universal, yet morally significant for the effect they affect, as a result of human will, desire, & principles of relationship, as opposed to... avarice & ill will.

Moon, as a part of the process of socializing members into integrating a more challenging moral compass & outlook on life, the past failures in history, with its variously socially significant actors, focused members on the relationship between Cain, Abel & God, as one of the most significant groupings, for its cumulative social impact. The 1st recorded murder offers much grist for reflection when encountered as a restorational opportunity gone real south of the border.

When completely understood, those few words of Moon mirrored Jesus' own words. But in such form as to offer a personal, public & political standard for engaging relationships that was ONLY matched by Jesus.

Mohammed, Buddha, Camus, King, Gandhi, spiritual teachers, parents... all advocated the same message... with one distinct difference.

ONLY Moon & Jesus demanded an absolute, single standard. The ONLY standard any 'true' parent would NATURALLY demand of their children.

Yet, in this, ONLY Moon & Jesus offered that this was the ONLY means to repair everything we had created. The ONLY means to a full & operational restoration of human potential. To the challenge posed by & in history, Jesus & Moon insisted that ALL be offered... or expect nothing. For nothing will have been offered.

Both stipulated that 'heaven' was merely a sustained state of such a quality of interpersonal relationships, that we could live for eternity with such a state, as THE state that defines the 'who,' 'what', & 'how' we are, with all others. And thus, they with us.

Heaven, on earth, or in some imagined after life, is defined by BOTH Jesus & Moon as the co-creation of a then grateful humanity, gratitude the motives informing all human intercourse.

ONLY in such a state is a full engagement of the potential of relationship with God now fully possible. Much less, only in such a state will human relationships reach their own fulfillment, as a matter of living, even if the issue of an eternity is to be addressed.

But for human history, it is the day to day that consumes us, & thus, needs our attendance & restoration.

It is here that ONLY Moon & Jesus ultimately establish their credentials & natural authority.

For while neither attended any accredited school for the material they offer, as their statement of beingness, this is the 'wisdom' of a life lived that they witness to, as their success.

They reveal that we will properly learn HOW to live WITH humanity, as a moral statement of integration &

community, when the informing values will produce THAT fruit are chosen & lived.

But we do not observe a world where Jesus' & Moon's words are revealed as some social norm.

Why?

Because, as yet, we do not understand what role they HAD to play, to be a true child of God. We do not understand the 'heart', the core of their messages. In failing thus, we find no one who offers the same message, even amongst their own disciples.

ONLY Moon's wife has exhibited the same values, the same understanding.

Today, in this book, I seek to reintroduce humanity to Jesus & Moon. Two brothers, who reveal their kinship in the ONLY way Jesus offered that was both natural to being human, but also the ONLY path to such personal restoration that we naturally emerge as the children of God, fully mature.

WHAT ESTABLISHED & ESTABLISHES THE UNIQUENESS OF BOTH JESUS & MOON IS WHAT DEFINED THEM AS FULLY HUMAN, FULLY MATURE, IN EVERY ASPECT NEEDED BY HUMANITY; THIS TO JUSTIFY OUR EXISTENCE AS 'WORTHY' TO THE TASK OF NOT JUST LIVING AS A CONSUMER, BUT ACTING AS THE PINNACLE OF CREATION, WHO SHARES IN THAT CREATION IN THE NATURE OF THE CO-CREATED EFFORT WE BRING TO BEAR, TO LIFE & LIVING.

This to be OUR living legacy; humanity, integrated into a quality of living gratitude, for life & its opportunities, the final witness as to the creative perfection of the cosmos...

Join me then, as we explore what it meant… & means… 'to be human,' being human.

Many sought to teach us, to guide us.

ONLY 2 gave us ALL we needed… to be human.

ONLY 2 offered ONLY a 'true parent's heart.'"

Introduction

"Houston, we have a problem": The global family social protests seek our universal conscience & heart & Jewish history responds

"For I dipt into the future, far as human eye could see...
Saw the Vision of the world & all the wonder that would be..."
Tennyson

"It's been a long, a long time coming... but I know a change is
gonna come...yes it is." Sam Cooke

"All disorder in the kingdom has the same explanation. When
we examine into the cause of it, it is found to be the want of
mutual love." Mo Tzu

"When one truly loves, it means that there is always a common
base from which to bond with others... naturally leading to
integration & sustainable community." The Last Spiritual
Samurai

"As I live, says the Lord God, I have no pleasure in the death
of the wicked." Ezekiel 33.11

"This is supposed to be a Christian nation, but tremendous damage has been done to the world... the good Christian moral & cultural tradition is gone... The Protestant & Catholic culture will never do for the future..." Rev. Sun Myung Moon

"When women are honored, there the gods are pleased; but where they are not honored, no sacred rite yields rewards." Hinduism

"When a foreigner resides among you in your land, do not mistreat them. The foreigner residing among you must be treated as your native born. Love them as yourselves, for you were foreigners in Egypt. I am the Lord your God." Leviticus 19:33-34

"No one of you is a believer until he loves for his brother what he loves for himself." Islam

"To live in an anti-racist society, we must collectively renew our commitment to a democratic view of racial justice & equality. Pursuing that vision, we create a culture where *beloved community* flourishes & is sustained. Those of us who know the joy of being with folks from all walks of life, all races, who are fundamentally anti-racist in their habits of being, need to give public testimony. We need to share not only what we have experienced, but the conditions of change that make such experience possible. The interracial circle of love that I know can happen because each individual present in it has made his or her own commitment to living an anti-racist life... It is this generous spirit of affirmation that gives us the courage to challenge one another, to work through misunderstandings... In a *beloved community* solidarity & trust are grounded in profound commitment to a shared vision." Bell Hooks

"Be ye therefore perfect, as your father/parent in heaven." Jesus

The favorite excuse of ALL time? "NOBODY'S perfect!"

If that is available as anybody's legitimate excuse, then all history must be forgiven.

Christians have allowed a 'success at failure' to become the distinguishing moral statement of their history, from Paul to this day. Marking time, allowing a false understanding of Jesus, his words & self-assumed mission, have allowed a degree of freedom most un-Christian. A degree of freedom sought & taken.

Under the false tutelage of Paul's limited & limiting understanding of Jesus, a global corporation was created that became the model for all the worst behaviors of capitalism.

Rather than teaching the elements of The True Family Values, that defined Jewish history in particular, &

human history in general, Christianity became the model for all forms of self-serving efforts to persuade, dominate & guilt shame people into both surrender, submission & social & political compliance, the first step to slavery of any variety, mental or physical, & establishing a 'natural' moral right to the wealth of others. Such wealth being intellectual, emotional, psychological, spiritual or physical.

The result of this most egregious misunderstanding of Christianity's proper mission & role, was that all the 'rights' now defended by our social consciences & social activists, especially those involving racism, sexism & environmental abuse & misuse, are now NOT defended as a true family norm, a global standard that EVERY family, of ANY religious or ideological persuasion, could embrace as natural & needed, is instead offered as 'impossible'.

What are these 'rights?'

Rights, as an individual & global social issue, are expressed as such because of human history. For the suffering that has been imposed, by others, upon the unwilling, only for the fact of insufficient means to correct or stop such abuse. Rights as articulated today merely embrace all the natural & normal behaviors even ideal people would manifest, much less the 'least' of us.

For simply, what is demanded in all cases is that a proper morally significant standard of social civility is natural to what it must mean 'to be human'.

Jesus demanded that a proper faith honored the wishes of God, a God assumed & defended as exposing the true heart of a parent towards all of humanity, not just 'the chosen'.

Even the idea of 'the chosen' has been perverted to mean anything, to anybody & everybody. The 'chosen' were actually like the 1st child in a family. That child, not by any virtue of any action or motive taken on its own behalf, is given the 'traditions' of the family to learn, hence, the 1st to be honored as a 'child' of that family, of those parents.

The 'justification' of being honored as the 1st though is 'earned' in the trenches of living, in all its full color. The learning curve is steep, fraught with errors of judgement, some of which, as a matter of our use of true freedom, is delayed as a rational cognitively available socially significant understanding. This because fully rational uses of freedom are as yet beyond the capacity of any child to grasp. This because the reasoning part of the brain is just now developing, hence some of the capacity to understand 'why' is naturally delayed.

Even though such maturity is in part a physiological development, it has its social consequences. In the meantime, parent's values, both personal, & as they are interpreted in the public & political arenas, come into play in both the socialization of 'expectations' as to obedience & then, its natural evolutionally expression of maturing, cooperation.

It is this 'maturing' of understanding as to the importance of the values that inform our motives for integration & community, that family comes into its own, both for its value to community & its moral authority, that is rooted as much in the heart of the offered & sustained experiences of care & attendance, as in any needs to obey & cooperate.

Regardless, for every parent, the child who deviates from such norms as is important to any in the community, this child no less than any other, is thus exposed to forgiveness, as a living interpersonal strategy, brought to bear to aid the child in their own restorative efforts. This offering the child the sense of the proper social & personal significance & needed order to relationships, but also of forgiveness & repentance as natural social skills, to be mastered in their own use.

The 1st child always makes it easier for the second child to get into the community thing quicker. First, there is the natural sense of community that emerges between peers, in this case, children. Trust & mimicry are natural, making the learning curve still just as real, but potentially much less to learn through experiences & any resulting mistakes or harms that might result from the early uses of freedom.

Had the values that defined the moral order of the Jewish culture, that define & legitimize Jesus in his environmental & global moral significance, had these values defined Jewish life, not just as offered in its emotional & spiritual state of mind, then families all over the world would have had the exposure to such an interpersonal value orientation & paradigm. EVERY moral teacher in history, worth their salt, defined & defended the quality of values that determine the very core of The True Family Values.

As you wander the pages of this manuscript, you will observe two things. #1 & MOST significant?

All the true moral teachers of history have defended The True Family Values & they offer a variety of such supports most of us have not been exposed to. These then are the authenticators of the final conclusion offered by Jesus & later articulated & defended again in such perfect form as Jesus stipulated to, by Sun Myung Moon.

Hence, Jesus & Moon BOTH enter our homes, not as intruders, seeking to dominate & control us, making us some form of 'Christian' to suit the masses of such people, but rather they enter our homes through our own sacred teachers. Reflected in our own choices of values lived & defended. Supported by those around us.

Our own teachers offer us the wisdom of their own reflected upon experiences. They concur with Jesus & Moon, each & everyone. But strangely, none are required to give up anything, or take anything but the message, to be lived.

Hence, even as Christianity has failed in its own personal, & therefore public mission, each of us have been exposed to the values that define The True Family Values.

We also choose how much to care... or more to the point, how little we will morally hold ourselves accountable to what we all know is truth... relationships matter & the ONLY path to the healthy version for humanity requires more than a casual investment of heart & will.

Yet, today we stand at what appears to be a cliff's edge.

The solution sought in history, paradoxically, was revealed in history. Our history. Human history, by humans.

But it requires we confront the 'man in the mirror.' Just how 'human' do we imagine we want to be? We've ALL seen & experienced, first hand, the values that have been the global standard for a LONG time now. They ain't working for us.

But human history has a surprise.

Those answers? Ah, shucks, we knew it all along. We just needed to be as desperate as we are to finally get humble enough to cry out for help!

Who's gonna help us?

We are. Starting by understanding the uniqueness of Jewish history, that speaks for humanity as to our needs, & our conclusions. Whether God was a social agent in this process or it's the result of human moral & psychological evolution, read finally maturing, the result & value of Jewish history, to all humanity, the past & the present, & to the Jewish people themselves, is absolute.

It just asks the final question… do you really wanna care?

If not… remember the Dodo.

If our choice is WITH history, then we will join our Jewish family, our social protestors, get our hearts out & dust them off & then, renew our convictions, as to our own worth… & every other person we must share this home with.

With Jewish history revealed, with a social conscience in tune with human need & potential, nothing can stop humanity… from caring.

As a religious narrative, or as a secular narrative, the development of human history is reflected in the evolving values that demand community, beloved community, as its natural state.

It is either a return to original values that define & defend such community or we need to advance in our heart of desire to seek such wisdom. Values that do not inherently lead to harm.

Those values the 'birth' of human harm & integrative failure.

Conclusion…

There are 2 main morally significant movements in human history. They are philosophically, morally & psychologically at odds with one another. The one the antithesis of the other.

One seeks domination, subjugation, marginalization, surrender, & even, isolation of others. These have the 'natural' tendency to create social & environmental slavery. This is obvious in such forms as capitalism, communism, racism, sexism, environmental exploitation. It is the cry of the anarchist, the absolutist immoralist who embraces only its own morality. Such people imagine themselves the 'chosen'. God's elect. The morally superior, the 'entitled,' by merely being alive. The consumer of relationships.

The other school of being recognizes community as the perfect environment for individuality to emerge, as a sacred entity. The 1st community being family, all subsequent communities merely the variant echoes of this foundational, intergeneration social system. This system recognizes the innate value & wisdom of relationships, to not only human survival, but also contributing to the quality of experience & opportunity for creative self-expression it naturally provides.

This is the school of thought that recognizes the sacred value of life. Then, imagines the human moral equivalent for engagement by humanity itself.

Here we encounter the Gandhi's, the Prophet, Jesus, Rosa Parks & so many others. Even ourselves, on a good day. But…

It will become obvious as we proceed here that Christianity never truly inherited either the words of life offered by Jesus, as the conclusion of God's dialogue with humanity. They never understood the 1st son of Israel any more than their predecessors, the Jewish people. We all suffer for this, we all adding our own bad histories to that which proceeded us.

Both groups missing the message; the Christians for their arrogance of personal salvation, of a kind & quality never offered by Jesus, & the Israelites for their failure to understand their own history & its intercessor & that specific agenda. But failures easily fallen into. Yet, when all is considered...

Both failed to live the words of advice offered.

Both communities were, & more importantly, are still commissioned to love God with all their hearts, minds & souls. THAT commandment did not cease to call our hearts to their proper attendance & self-nurturing loving behavior.

IF we imagine we are to be measured as true children of God, as Jew or Christian, that is.

No other community of faith or life meaning has offered greater wisdom than was offered these two communities. Both sharing one lineage, established & secured by one faithful child.

Today, no community rises to the anguished call of humanity, for peace.

Yet, as we will discover, it is all here... we have been properly gifted. We have been loved beyond imagination, whether it was God or history.

But we recognize neither the gift, nor the gifter.
THAT MUST BE REMEDIED.
The 'gift' is the means out of our created hell.

Chapter 1 - Listening as our 1st humility & the 'Zen' of freedom: The witness & wisdom of the cosmos vs human truth & knowledge

"It may be displeasing to religious believers, especially to Christians, to learn that a new expression of truth must appear. They believe that the scriptures they have are already perfect & flawless... Scriptures... are not the truth itself, but are textbooks teaching the truth." Rev. Sun Myung Moon's Exposition of the Divine Principle

"The 2nd course of human endeavor is the attempt to answer the fundamental questions about human life by transcending the resultant world of phenomena & searching for the world of essence." Rev. Sun Myung Moon's Exposition of the Divine Principle

"Sociology... is a science which attempts the interpretive understanding of social action in order thereby to arrive at a causal explanation of its course & effects. In 'action' is included all human behavior when & in so far as the acting individual attaches a subjective meaning to it. Action in this sense may be either overt or purely inward or subjective; it may consist of positive intervention in a situation, or of deliberatively refraining from such intervention or passively acquiescing in the situation. Action is social in so far as, by virtue of the subjective meaning attached to it by the acting individual (or individuals), it takes into account of the behavior of others & thereby is oriented in its course." Max Weber

In a previous religious association, our introductory lectures often included an 'elephant' story. In this story, many blind people encounter the elephant, each describing their own 'insight' into the form of the beast. Of course, the point being two-fold. THEY could ONLY know partial truths... while, of course, 'WE' KNEW ALL SIGNIFICANT TRUTH TO KNOW, IE, THE TRUTH THEY NEEDED.

A greater problem for humanity are the sheer numbers & the varieties of 'truth' & the standards they reveal, that are beyond our capacity to truly digest & gain wisdom from. There are even 'untruths' paraded as 'truth.' The flat earth people. A president who had an election stolen.

Fake & false truths & inspiration surrounds us. Seek to dominate us, influence & control us, take from us & make us grateful for the opportunity.

But we do not yet recognize the critical wisdom that may be universally accessible. OUR needed wisdom.

In the world, in a variety of forms to stagger the imagination, there is 'men's' truth, offering a rationale & justification for men to imagine themselves as different, & superior, to women. An example that sorely begs the questions... "is THIS the truth we need? If not, what 'truth' DO we need?"

We also discover there is religious truth, personal truth, national truths, cultural truths, racial & ethnic truths. Maybe even you have some special truth we are yet to share.

But the 'truth' we REALLY need?

How to live with ourselves so that we desire to live with each other... & are willing to inherit & employ the values needed for that success.

It is time for humanity to mature... to own its place in the sun. By how we create, with each other, the ecology needed to support all humanity, as a family. This then the environment we offer to the cosmos of the commitment & the quality of commitment we have made to ourselves, by how we will engage the totality of the cosmos.

All other 'truth' melts into the sun of relativity & context to require their particular presences.

It was a sad moment when one day I had to confront members from that previous association, that their interpretation that THEY & THEY ALONE had knowledge & possession of all most significant 'truths' & as such, ONLY THEY knew the 'elephant' that all the rest of us were blind about, & thus only partially perceiving, was in FACT, in error.

Actually, quite a fatal error.

Its evidence is the current sundering of the association into competing organizations. This lack of critical understanding... the glue to all true relationships.

What was so sad is their refusal to accept that the cosmos might have more than just 'THEIR' knowledge to impart, including such new, globally significant history & its liberating message; such history now as to offer a needed correction for ALL humanity to consider, needing to commence immediately. A course correction requiring a new state of mind, of heart.

Wisdom offered & wisdom refused is madness. Hence, those who thought they knew the elephant, were the blind leading the blind. Good hearts... but lost to reality...

63

It is one creature to 'know' something to be true & quite another critter to know 'why' it is true. To understand not just its external & obvious meaning to any particular audience, but, more to the point, 'why' such 'truth' IS important, or should be considered as critically important to us.

The most profound example of such a state of confusion is one that has existed for 2000 years.

Namely... WHY WAS JESUS THE MESSIAH?

Oh, sure, AFTER his death, his death was falsely used to mislead generations away from the REAL Jesus. Adherents falsely claiming that the mere 'belief' in Jesus as a messiah was enough to inherit all the benefits such belief would not only warrant, but actually be so arrogant to offer an unconditional guarantee, one they cannot fulfill nor prove.

Jesus' words provide 'life' in the use WE assume to engage them with. WE GIVE LIFE, & THEREFORE, WITNESS, TO THE WORDS OF LIFE IN OUR OWN BEHAVIOR.

Even Satan recognized Jesus as messiah.

Didn't affect him in the least. So we are told. Look around.

He just wouldn't 'do' as Jesus offered the true children of God could... & would offer.

In a similar fashion, those who purport to have some needed 'truth' available no-where else, often introduces the 'elephant' story. Here, we discover we, & most other people, only partially experience the 'elephant of truth & reality' whereas our revelator offers us what no others can.

The complete picture.

How real is this dilemma?

When I offered new revelations about the God of Jew, Christian & Muslim, not one person in hundreds cared to explore its possibility with me, even when I offered it provided a quality of proof for the existence of God unparalleled anywhere. This with my own religious community.

When I offered select people the 'proof' that science now provides for some of their most cherished religious myths, NOT ONE was interested.

Why?

They already had 'all the truth,' or at least all the truth they think they needed.

How far off they were & are is of social significance, one now unavoidable. For others.

This was their cherished use of freedom.

Now, it might seem I have thus just set myself up for the same judgement.

In a sense, I have.

But what I seek to offer is only what has been bequeathed to me, that must be shared.

The cosmos & Jesus… & now Moon, have all argued but one point.

The individual & collective significance of relationships, to life, its continued existence… & to the quality of that experience & its development.

As we forge ahead, individually & as nationals & as global citizens, it is critical we evolve past the arrogance of such exclusivity, that the Tower of Babel is the ONLY course ahead.

Me & 'my' truth to the exclusion of you & 'your' truth.

We MUST come to a consensus of need & viable means of not just conflict management, but more to the point, its elimination as such a compelling factor of daily human life & living.

The cosmos, however we imagine its origin, has provided but one witness & one alone. The social significance of relationships.

From the simple atom, to the human eye, to the human body as a totality of potential, the cosmos reveals a 'wisdom' unparalleled for its significance not only to human life, but the quality of life we may create for ourselves.

Here is a simple statement of the cosmos that is available to all humanity to grasp & integrate into their conscious awareness &… conscience, too.

The 1st Wisdom: The cosmic significance of interpersonal relationships

The 1st Wisdom of Relationships: Integration is the key to sustainable life

The 2nd Wisdom of Relationships: Relationships are about transformation of existing resources & 'social agents' into a particular quality of community, marked by its degree of integration, & hence, rationally accessible moral conceptualizations are revealed in the nature of the integration & its resultant 'creation'.

The 3rd Wisdom of Relationships: Relationships…
THIS IS THE PURPOSE OF LIFE

The 4th Wisdom of Relationships: Conflict, like a wound to the body, is communication to be taken seriously.

The Final Wisdom of Relationships: Maturity, as the natural behavioral measurement of human social value & status, is only realized in morally significant sustainable community. The human creation of a 'social form of sustainable life.' In this, then humanity, in the use of reason & the will to care, replicates the very nature & form of the cosmos in its creation of life.

If the creation, without mind or hand, can create mind & hand, then maybe we need to listen, take note, seek wisdom, & then, & only then, act.

Chapter 2- Defining a rationale for human nature: Honoring the universal significance of relationships

"The significance of relationships is the core to human happiness no less than our survival & to the quality of that survival. Until we accept the universal need for psychologically healthy relationships, that are foundationally established in the family, in the principles each family has mastered & can give experience to, both experientially as well as cognitively, there is no hope for community, much less peace." The Last Spiritual Samurai

"Here then is the origin & rise of government; namely a mode rendered necessary by the inability of moral virtue to govern the world..." Thomas Paine

"Primary among the resources available to the human quest are, of course, those features of its own nature that best equip it to respond to the obstacles met in living. The advancement of these characteristics constitutes the evolutionary development of *homo sapiens*. If we can identify these features, we will have located the evolutionary ground of moral value; for such attributes are valuable precisely because they are essential to the continuance & extension of humanity. An individual cannot aim his/her conduct at the survival of the species, but one CAN aim at nurturing those natural capacities upon which species survival depends." Christopher Lyle Johnstone

"When women are honored, there the gods are pleased; but where they are not honored, no sacred rite yields rewards." Hinduism, Laws of Manu

"The whole of the Torah is for the purpose of promoting peace." Judaism, Talmud, Gittin 59b

"The Master said, "When we see men of worth, we should think of equaling them; when we see men of a contrary character, we should turn inwards & examine ourselves." Confucius

"Tsze-kung asked, saying, "Is there one word which may serve as a rule of practice for all one's life?" The Master said, "Is not RECIPROCITY such a word? What you do not want done to yourself, do not do to others." Confucius

"Those of us who are not cynical, who still cherish the vision of *beloved community*, sustain our conviction that we need such bonding not because we cling to utopian fantasies but because we have struggled all our lives to create this community... Even though that commitment was first made in the mind, it is realized by concrete action, by anti-racist living & being... The small circle of love we have managed to form in our individual lives represent a concrete realistic reminder that *beloved community* is not a dream, that it already exists for those of us who have done the work of educating ourselves for critical consciousness..." Bell Hooks

When we settle back & observe 'what is', ask the 'right' questions, then listen, we discover much more is available to us than if we merely bluff it out, guess, & hump it.

If the cosmos 'wisdom' is the creation of sustainable life & IF that success means anything to us, as reflective creatures utilizing our uniquely rational brains, then we have our 1st "ah hah!" moment.

If relationships are 'all that' & more, then we, in our own exercise of wisdom, add that factor to the equation that holds us all together, friend & enemy alike.

Our enemy is the 'master' of such knowledge, that little piece the means to their 'way of being,' as our enemy. When we choose to harm, we have honored the social significance of relationships, as the unwitting vehicle & servant to all they MUST serve.

Relationships are the 1st slaves to the evil that men do. Then, the people in them are the next slaves to evil.

70

First, we debase the obvious. We trash the potential for relationship. Then we proceed to make it personal.

Now, in some fanciful drama, we imagine mere civility is enough these days. Enough in the offering, enough in the expectations of others.

If I lose it at times, if I can't really bring myself to care more than I do, then I am actually pretty much indistinguishable to any others.

We make excuses.

We declare, with some authority, that "nobody's perfect" & then march forth righteous in our 'wisdom.'

Yet, given the personal & universal significance of relationships, to life itself & the quality of life experienced, then the first glimmer of wisdom is when we set ourselves to the task, as a sincere effort, to redefine the challenge before humanity so that our effort is properly guided towards the personal, public & political goals we seek for relationships.

We KNOW the challenge emerges in relationships. They emerge BECAUSE of the values that inform both our motives & the choices we then employ.

Hence, we realize that the values chosen, consciously or not, are part of the root cause. So, human freedom & peace is being adversely affected by our use of our freedom. Also, the values we assume are our 'right' to employ in relationships are part of the source problem, too. Freedom in the variety of values available as options is then also of concern.

We seek peace.

We seek community, as a healthy experience & as the ONLY means to civilization & family health.

Then, it is in the choice of informing values, our commitment to them, as a sustained act of freedom, & the social breadth of application needed then that is the task before us.

Between this hard place & the reality of human harm that is sustained in every way, we are left at the footsteps of a need for values that encourage the most perfectly sustainable human investment. A quality of values that inherently demands integration, not as a force of law, but of the heart, of the human nurtured & natured will to care.

We observe, first in the family, the generalized & greatest commitments to family & individuals offered across all cultures, ethnicities & races. It is from this reservoir of sustained experience in history that we discover the ONLY human roots that can offer us not just hope, but practical moral opportunity.

We know that parents offer a quality of sustained commitment to their children & each other, that allows a degree of freedom & community to exist & potentially prosperity not possible any other way.

We are beginning to listen now.

We link that with the 'wisdom' of the cosmos & we find ourselves at door number 1. Relationships matter.

Hence, both as a physical wisdom & as a matter of human interest, relationships matter.

Conclusion, people matter.

Final wisdom: we need the moral paradigm that both honors individual & freedom; allowing a totality of autonomy & creative opportunity, that also secures community, for both parties. As a sustainable reality.

Even more… we now realize how much we need & can benefit each other.

The doors of perception are opening our mind's heart… that part of us we have nurtured to care beyond self-interest.

When we do, we find each other.

Now, what will we choose to do?

Repeat 6000 years of bloody history or venture into new territory.

That is why we are here now, together. To decide that very issue.

We choose... to be part of the solution.

But it will need be in the light of day, when reality most strikes at the heart of our idealism, that idealism not yet anchored in our total commitment to caring... bar none.

Hence, we need each other, too.

We have each other, as our 2nd selves. The resources are available, we need to gather to create a sustainable environment.

Then, the witness to the interpersonal value of True Family Values emerge, as the seed & the fruit, to the community we all know is possible.

In this, we co-create, with the cosmos, through such use of our bodies, the quality of interpersonal relationship that is needed to convince an apathetic & uncaring world... that they matter, too.

It is in this experience of the potential of relationship, even with those in conflict, that we realize the importance of the values we choose & then live by.

When we order our hot dog, we want the whole works. It's not just what 'might' taste good, it is what will make it the 'best' it can be...

It's what we want for all others.

WE BECOME THE SEED EXPERIENCE FOR OTHERS, OF THE BEST DAMN DOG ANYWHERE...

Chapter 3- Establishing a human vocabulary: relational maintenance & building bridges of 'heart' meaning to community

"I say what I mean & I mean what I say..."

"... the supreme end of man's vocation, sociability."
Immanuel Kant

"But communists, fascists, terrorists of all ilk, domestic & foreign, Nazi's & American racist white nationalists, all worship the same god... choose who & what you hate, then proceed to destroy what you hate, by any means possible. Hence, never admitting that while the opposite side is the enemy, as communist encounters white nationalist, they agree on one thing... the tools to persuade, that begin with hateful rhetoric, end with bullets. That is our challenge. To restore True Family Values to even the last of such anarchists. To restore true love." The Last Spiritual Samurai

The term 'nigger' has gone through many changes, many meanings. In time, I realized that while not black, many assumed to imagine me & treat me no differently than toward those the term was subsequently intended to be used against. I knew what every person learns in its use. It is a term of hate, of refusal to imagine that the being in front of us is worthy of being loved... or even loved by.

Even with the diversity of uses the term has been put to, today, because of the 'heart' of its original 'lay' & primary users, the word, in its use, is the antithesis of meaning anything human. The historical quality of heart mustered by its abusers force us this day to remember how words not only inform our behaviors, they form our histories, establish the witness to what we hold sacred... & what & those we do not.

Thanks to the universal nature of the employed values, even a white boy like me can experience all the same meanings, just expressed & justified to fit "my" situation.

If at birth, your own mama don't want to own you in her heart, cannot & will not, you know what it means to be a 'nigger'. Nobody has to call you the name. It is inscribed on your heart, the day you realized who didn't love you... nor wanted nor intended to. As a child, it is hard to recover from that insight. There is no refuge, no shelter from the elements, no safe harbor, no welcoming arms.

You are alone.

When you're a child, that's a bit to digest. No skill set in place.

Get over it... cause now you got to survive...

How strange it is, that we need to imagine a 'new' vocabulary to communicate with one another.

But my suggestion is even more radical. We need to develop this vocabulary for our own benefit first. The words we use, they carry weight beyond imagination.

They strike our memories, forcing to consciousness or the mere subconscious, biases from past experiences & thinking. The words we use may be specific to the past, to misuse then & now. We may enjoin meanings not owned or specific to our own experiences, biases & values, owned or not conscious.

Our vocabulary is our means to reach out to the world. Hence it is very 'us' specific.

In a world of evil, of uncaring motives & informing values, the words used would reveal at least two truths. They both hide & reveal, & they do so intentionally & unintentionally. Words are also used for their intended persuasive effect.

Persuasion is the effort to artificially 'force' a decision in favor of a predetermined outcome. Persuasion is seldom neutral, the desire forcing a motive & excess effort to gain support for one's favored position. The outcome to persuasion is seldom of an equality of benefit. Persuasion, by its very nature, does not require & is seldom aided by a revealing of all the factors coming into play with persuasive efforts. Persuasion seeks to dominate the moment, its actors & its outcome.

Persuasion, even for good cause, is a self-serving form of intercourse. In a truly loving community persuasion is not used, but rationality & reason itself. For what is truly good need only be offered as such. The rational, reasonable, caring human needs no more than such care to make informed & moral decisions.

To imagine a different world, we also need a corresponding vocabulary & rhetorical paradigm for creating sustainable community, especially 'beloved' community.

In each book prior to this, a vocabulary section was also established. It is not meant to be exhaustive, 'perfect', complete or without any error.

My effort is merely intended as a beginning point, given my research into what others meant & intended we inherit. I realized current rhetoric is hostile to the values of true love communities & THEIR communication needs & strategies for relationship building, as a foundation for a psychologically healthy culture & civilization to emerge. That serves ALL humanity, not just portions. Like the wealthy & those with power to 'force'.

Even our economics is tainted, capitalism offering its own vocabulary & rhetoric to support its undying demand for ongoing profit. From ANY source, human or not, cooperatively or not.

Please join me as we explore words for the value added support they can render to our decisions to care more, to care more substantially & to care as a sustainable social reality. Not the end all, but a good beginning point for further reflection & discussion. A place to start off together.

The True Family Values... understanding God's/cosmos' means to sustainable life

True Family Values are the experience of God, translated for & applied to human experience, potential & need. Love its priming symbol.

'Love' is that initial commitment to care, beyond self-interest... the all of who & what I am, as I offer to community. The substance of what it means 'to love' embedded in consequent behaviors, sustained over time. Love is the rational decision we make as to the principles that will inform & guide our interpersonal intercourse, of any kind & of any duration.

The following principles, or values, to guide interpersonal behavior, form the only needed core foundation for all subsequent social values to be defined by. They are the required social responses, both as strategy

& as means, to confront & integrate all deviating behaviors into a restorational posture, ready for human engagement.

Forgiveness… offering the 'deviant' our now contextually formed & sustained effort 'to love', to aid others in their conflict & disassociation… & their need for restoration to community. Forgiveness is merely the contextual reapplication of the original rational intent & heart to the current condition of relationships.

Repentance… an ultimate form of rationality, a chosen freedom, restoring self-love when so engaged as to offer to restore & morally participate in such offering to co-create beloved community. Repentance is movement towards reintegration.

These 3 'values', that also operate as principles to define our social strategy for integration & community formation, form the cognitively recognizable values ANY parent needs, to raise children to be properly motivated social agents & community members.

The True Family Values are the cognitively available human understanding of both the nature of the values that informed God's integrative efforts with humanity & the quality of attendance offered in such behavior, that are then framed in such rational terms correlative to human experience, need & potential, as individuals, families & as a species, as to then realize community.

Their content, as we need to consider, as a cognitive enterprise to be shared across all mediums, deserve more than the cursory brush offered in history & thus, we will deal with their more specific foundational considerations, in an initial effort to deconstruct the term, later in the thesis.

Conscience & heart... the process of maturing, by way of freedom

Conscience must be understood as the effect of the cultural training & choices we have established as having a compelling presence in our lives, in the moral formation of our public identity & interpersonal persona. Conscience is first natured & nurtured in the family, or whatever social agency is raising the children. Conscience is the social awareness & commitment we bring to the social environment, in the considerations given to the nature of & content of our socially significant behaviors. The conscience, as a social measure of our commitment to community, then consistency as a moral force will be determined both by the exposure as children to such influences that inspire a natural surrendering to such authority, as to assume its priorities & social norms, & those choices made consciously & unconsciously, as acts of maturing wisdom. Which are merely normative social habits forming as a matter of integration & conformity.

Conscience is then the social realization of our commitment to community, the link between our commitment to ourself, as an individual, & as our commitment to that same person, but now recognizable in community, as a sacred act of offering ourselves to act beyond mere self-interest. Conscience is the public face of our heart of hearts, those values we hold to & seek to protect, even hide from the public. When heart, conscience & desire for relationship as a sustained effort of discipline, with God &/or the environment, are unified morally, then we have a form of internal order that then places our emotional identity under the authority of that conscience, as the measure of our commitment to ourselves.

Our emotional impulses & inspirations will then naturally move us towards community, beloved community. Emotions offering a contextually significant 'meaning' to our acts, as well as the residual impact they effect on our consciousness.

Emotions are to be the servant of the body, not the end all of our choices as we enter the public arena. If they improperly dominate, the tendency then becomes, because of habit, immaturity, a lack of true family values, both as idea & experience, we will allow those emotional impulses to dominate, never to be challenged. 'How' we feel & why comes to dominate our world. But if the commitment is not to move beyond self-interest, then the heart is thrust aside, the conscience silenced... & hell is created.

The only true means then to the maturity we all seek & need is when our desire for interpersonal relationship is coupled with the quality of values that ALWAYS points true north. Towards community. Then, the temptations of bodily distractions, even of pain & suffering no less than those that are self-indulgent & not compatible with community, will not suffice to distract us & lead to undesired consequences.

Heart is the substance of what I truly have committed to care about. Discipline its greatest admirer & supporter. Heart being the depth I have imagined relationships to be, of a determined & sustained importance, the conscience then is its social application. Together, they are the witness to the world of the who we are, how we are & what we are, as we enter the social arena with its differing moral landscapes.

Then, we emerge. The creation we offer to the world.

Listening VS hearing... investing in our shared environment

In time, as we mature, we discover unconsciously that the quality of investment we make when we listen is refined, expanded & further offered as a social measure of our commitment to care. Listening is the active aspect of integration offered to others, establishing the public witness & experience that is critical to community, to be established, sustained & further developed as opportunity & need would offer is wisdom.

In contrast, hearing is the physical exercise of placing meaning to such events as to note our need &/or opportunity for response. Hearing requires no moral interpretation, no moral measurement as to the need for intervention, community or even response. Listening implies a moral investment is made, in the quality of care invested & sustained.

Listening is a form of preamble to community. Hearing just is.

Relational maintenance... sustaining the 'we are' in health

You check the oil in the car? You check wear & tear on the tires? Put in gas as needed, check-ups? That is your portion of offering to relational maintenance, that expresses your desire & care for & about that car. That continued effort allows a degree & quality of security & peace of mind not obtainable any other way, such that we then can drive around without much more thought about it all.

If we fail to sustain such effort?

Repairing the vehicle may not be a remaining option...

Citizen VS Patriot... children VS Parentism

It may seem stark & unfair to compare citizenship to being a child, but in a very real way, that is exactly the distinction that must be made, for any true progress to be made in what we will define as 'human' & defend as human. Children, until they begin to mature in their social understanding of both the necessity of relationships, but also for their potential for human specific meaning, value & potential for creating prosperity, will mostly act as consumers, doing little to add to the resources of the family or acting in its management & allocations. As children mature, that is integrate in such form as to become an asset to the family, both in the use of resources & in their allocation, children 'recognize' the 'value' of such behaviors & seeking to be a part of the family & with such guidance towards community as are needed by the parents, children begin to emerge as 'defenders' of that social group in their way of seeking to contribute, rather than just consume.

This is the movement of a citizen towards becoming a patriot. The patriot defends the values of the nation (social group) as not just a moral responsibility, but as a matter of the commitment one has offered oneself to. The patriot no longer first considers themselves & their needs & wants, but assumes a stewardship for the social environment shared, including its native resources as well as those garnered from outside the family. This to include all forms of resources, including economic as well as psychological.

The psychological element most effected & determinative for the child in the values of integration experienced & taught. Do they lead to a sense of both the sacred value of oneself, but only in the context of a greater whole, that embraces all with the same informing values? This is a foundation for a personal & social security that will serve a lifetime.

In maturing, the child, as a citizen of the family, just like the patriot, comes to live for their own family, & in time, recognizes other families for the same value. Hence, supports other families in like manner as to how one has integrated into one's own native lands.

The citizen, the maturing child, comes to a sense of a bonding of heart, of oneself to the totality of the environment one lives in, & shares with others. This is the evolution of maturing, movement from consumerism to creationism.

Patriotism, as an effect, is the movement of an identity of self as a singularity, to one in which a unique identity is not just embraced, then nurtured in what is its natural environment, with its corresponding ecology... beloved community, but it is the corresponding living commitment to the health of that community.

In America, that definition of health was first imagined to require a moral state of awareness & commitment to "all are created equal," that a social state, a political environment, is created that can sustain a community of such individuals. This then producing a nation with a cosmic identity to be shared by all... even those beyond the nation's borders. ALL children of the same creator.

This 'heart of attendance,' embraces all the values of the true parent... hence, the result is the creation of 'parentism,' the political expression of True Family Values, offered to the social & political arenas in our behavior. Parentism, the ultimate form of stewardship.

Vulnerability…the rational choice allowing 'we are'

To establish the potential for relationships, whether they create true love relationships & community or not, requires an initial offering of 'trust'… or vulnerability. We place ourselves, in real time & proximity, to those we integrate with. This can be for a moment, or a lifetime.

When I open the door in public, acting to aid someone I do not know, I must submit to the requirement that I must care enough, either about the opportunity, or the person, or both, to choose to make such an offering. It may be rejected, deemed out of place, undesirable, for its source or purpose; the considerations involved may never be revealed or otherwise divulged, but my vulnerability expressed is the hand offered, open palm, revealing no weapon, no threat.

Vulnerability is a minimal requirement for any true civility, but for community to be created & sustained takes a greater effort & thus, revelation of self, situationally, but intimately so in time.

Hence, if one seeks to love, then this aspect of offering becomes natural, if always contextual. Vulnerability is like a surgeon preparing to aid another… integration the key, care for other the means, vulnerability, the opening of space to create, the operating room shared.

Intimacy… choosing our foundations & allowing 'skin touch'

Intimacy… perceived by many men as a natural threat. Why? Because we know we are all fakes, & with intimacy, too much is revealed, even if not everything. We men know we cannot keep up the façade of the gap between who we want you to imagine us as VS who we really are when we greet that person in the mirror each morning.

Yet, a healthy intimacy is both a natural condition to develop love, it is also its potential witness.

Intimacy allows both proximity & contextual opportunity for contact, physical or psychological/spiritual. Intimacy is offering made, not thought about as a profit/loss potential proposition. Intimacy assumes commitment.

Shame VS guilt… 'I offer' VS 'we take'

Shame is actually a good thing. Guilt is a different measure of the same event, as a moral consideration. Guilt is a 'quantity' that then demands a payment to indemnify, even if not to restore any aspect of the deviance, either for victim, or for deviant. Guilt is the measure of the 'evil' created that then needs compensation of some kind(s). Guilt is measured from outside the deviant, without aid from the deviant, except as legal remedies allows for a defense & advocacy against the interests of those arguing guilt exists & must be formally acknowledged & acted upon. Again, ultimately, with little freedom for remedy by the deviant themselves.

Shame, in contrast, is the rational realization of the gap between what is possible as a morally significant integration & what occurred. Shame is the rational acknowledgement that what transpired should not have, accepts & acknowledges alternative values & behaviors as what was required, by humanity, to be human.

Shame then acts as a social revelation of heart, of the desire for opportunity to restore the aggrieved past, by implementing an alternative set of values & hence, subsequent behaviors. Shame is the evidence of the effort to create anew… to re-create, but towards community establishment as to support beloved community.

Shame assumes a 'right' to corrective offerings… guilt seeks to hide from reality, fearing those with the power & motive to extract payment for offences, restoration not the central or even a proximate concern. One seeks restoration & freedom, the other fears, especially those then who would seek retribution & revenge, that one suffers for one's deviances. Shame may produce some measure of discomfort & painful offerings, but it is a measure of heart, hence, what is offered, can never be taken, merely received. Shame seeks restoration & community.

Shame rationally re-establishes our human priorities… we matter.

Integration… the measure of 'heart' offered, as sustainable behavior

The initial GREATNESS of America, in demanding that we honor each other as equal to ourselves, offers us the greatest inducement & greatest rewards at the same time. To co-create a sustainable, morally significant community of such individuals, never so gathered before in human history. Bequeathed with such opportunities that so many died for, so many dreamed of, so many never thought the day would come.

In such values are the greatest encouragement for a rational & yet, heartfelt gratitude. In such a declaration, our ancestors could 'look down' & observe that humanity has FINALLY matured enough to realize the personal & public significance of SHARING opportunities.

Integration is what children experience as they emerge into a social consciousness of both environment & actors. It becomes a matter of heart in time. It is sustained because of that heart, that desire & support for caring, both as a behavior, & as sought from the social actors themselves as motive for acting with each other.

Integration is the heart of community. It is the behavioral expression of desire & will for beloved community. It requires vulnerability & intimacy… as sustained offerings. This part of the 'glue.'

Freedom… so far, the playground is a bloody madman's dream

It seems no people, anywhere, have a very healthy notion of freedom, as it needs to be considered by humanity, to survive, not just to gain wisdom. Or even to justify any prosperity.

Freedom, now interpreted as the opportunity to act without regard for motive or consequence, is ONLY in the imagination of children & madmen. Both discover that freedom without moral concerns allows oneself to fully engage the moment. That seems like power… But we live in a world of consequence. It has meaning for humanity.

No one wants to be a victim.

Strangely, especially those who victimize.

Their own logic is the reason NOT to victimize.

It is never a good experience for somebody.

America offered a dream no where else offered in such form. The fundamental behaviors & the fundamental civil rights one needed, to be protected in & from history, were now not only articulated, but given such protection that only heaven could offer more. Freedom of religion, freedom of speech, press & association. Freedom from unprincipled searches, by government or brigand, would now be the letter of laws all are beholden to.

BUT... the wisdom of God, the wisdom of men, the wisdom of experience, whatever the source of inspiration, but the founders included one proviso that not only indicated the moral direction of the 'rights' now to be celebrated in behaviors, but, as patriots, that now, we needed to no less jealously act to protect our neighbor's opportunity, as much as we might seek to celebrate & protect our own opportunities.

Just like the maturing child that discovers their world includes such others, that one's own freedoms & opportunities all of a sudden seem limited & lost, or at least significantly diminished, the citizen must share the social environment that allows the engagement of all those wonderful & sacred behaviors.

Now, we must share the sandbox.

That redefines freedom.

Get it?

Freedom of speech... offering the 'treasures of the heart'

Today, speech is so assumed as a 'right' that it is given the same moral parameters children naturally do. None. Today, lies are touted as equal to truth, to be honored as if truth. Recognizing this timeless social reality, Jesus noted it was not that which went into our mouths that condemned us, but every word offered forth from our mouths, revealing the abundance of the heart & its intended degree & quality of sustained care offered. Jesus noted that our words revealed the treasures of our hearts. Or the lack of treasure.

He warned there was no grace given nor quarter offered for those who refused to care & would imagine themselves truly part of either the Jewish community, or more to the point, it directly affected the nature & quality of relationship possible with God. Hence, the moral justification for the prophets of old. Prophets, when embraced as social representative agents for God, were honored for their words… or if not honored, then victimized.

For the use of their words… to serve their God.

This sense of the sacred possibility of the use of words, has inspired revolutions, brought to light great potential wisdom for humanity… but also brought us to the point of potential extinction. What lesson is revealed in that stark reality?

Freedom/free will… the textual 'joy' of offering in America

One of the great misunderstanding of Americans, especially its Christian, white men, is the notion that America's 1st & most significant value is 'freedom'. Freedom is, 1st & foremost, from conception to execution, a matter of proper 'offering,' it is not about what one consumes or takes, as an assumed entitlement, or earned. Freedom ultimately is the revelation of what opportunities exist for me to act in a specific environment, in such form as to also naturally integrate with that environment & its ecological morality. Freedom, as a human recognized & demanded consideration, must always be considered as a contextual opportunity. All human harm originates in that 1st assumption, of a unique entitlement that allows one to act as an environmental terrorist. A terrorist in the failure to have any commitment to the greater 'whole' that is or will be affected, directly or collaterally.

In America, the 1st freedom, the freedom 'to be', is also the declaration of the 1st responsibility, whether one is a native or not. Honoring that ALL others are created equal, generates the foundation for a national community/family to be substantially established. The national standard for a generalized evolution of our social conscience was also then established, enshrined & continues to be realized, through our amendment process.

Men declared the 1st obligation as one that requires the very social reality needed to protect those with the least power; personal, public or political. IOW's, in declaring 'all are equal,' creates a social obligation to not only support that 1st virtue… or it judges us as 'unworthy,' in our step away from what it 'means' to be an American. Being born here is not just about entitlements. It is about recognizing my neighbor, as my 2nd self. The person, if that be me, that I want to have all the access to behaviors so controlled & denied in human history.

Hence, if one is grateful, for what one inherits & does not have to earn, then one honors that value with one's own pledge of filial piety. That is the joy of offering America provides ANYONE within these borders… the least as any, the criminal & the saint together. All the same opportunity. The freedom to offer & thus, establish not only personal significance, but to also support community in such form & way as to offer a light upon history, that what was, will be no more, for the living proof of what is possible. With heart, values & discipline of will…

The 3 Great Human Virtues… Remembering our common ancestors

When I discovered the core values that informed Jesus' understanding of God & human history, as I came to articulate it & differentiate them from other social values, I also discovered the kinship we all share with the Jewish people.

All our teachers, our prophets, our seers, our wisemen & mothers, all through history the words of 'love,' 'forgiveness' & 'repentance' surfaced in peoples minds…but then found community when rhetorically shared.

Gandhi, Camus, Paine, King, Rosa Parks… all these recent social activists called upon humanity to share one thing, & one thing only.

Ourselves… with each other.

THAT future, that inevitability, that hope has been expressed all through history.

But integration being the purpose, then ONLY those values supportive of that social proposition would be carried forward as the wisdom of our sages, the wisdom of our mothers, the wisdom of ages.

The 3 Great Human Virtues… as Jesus noted, there was no greater love than one offers one's life for the sake of another. This is the heart of every true parent, every true patriot. The derivative human values, that sustain family life, then became perpetuated as the 'norm' for strategies of continued efforts at integration & community creation.

These 'virtues' then are the cornerstone to not only any true civility & civilization, they are also the proper & best practices means for parents to socialize the next generation, to become the future patriot/parents. Then they form what we can understand as The True Family Values.

Timeless, to all peoples.

Faith… 'the conscious & purposed walk with'…

The notion of 'faith' as a living component of one's life emerged with Abraham & his understanding of God & what that god was requiring. Ultimately, because of the social/psychological state of humanity, as an anti-social creature that also needs relationships, & the corresponding needed commitment, humanity was no better off than a child in its capacity to understanding God's intents, behavior & expectation.

Faith became not only 'the walk with God,' as established with Abraham, but faith became the way I lived with others, as Moses established was God's will & wishes; this to honor 'OUR' relationships to God, as an individual & as a 'people.' With Moses, faith became 'how I walked with God, in my walk with you, my neighbor, or, in time, even my enemy'.

Today, faith is restored to 'how I walk with you, so we might walk with God, together.'

Emotions… a sacred servant, the means, not master, nor the ends

When we assume our emotions are the 'cats meow' in any we world we so choose, because we have chosen to insist that is what freedom will mean, we have retreated into childhood.

The body needs & uses emotions as a tool & aid.

As mentioned, emotions emerge out of a particular part of the brain, serving the body as an alerting system & motivator towards such social behavior as events & actors require, to defend oneself or to integrate. Emotions are like the best friend, they are always intimate & immediate, & while they may get upset with life & its actors, they are mostly 'right' about their own state. I feel, therefore I am right in those feelings.

Emotions always exist in an existential 'now'. They can be cultivated both by real world, immediately consuming events, or they can be stimulated by our choices or memories that rise up in response to events or reflection.

Emotions are not meant to dictate the nature of our integration into events, they act to serve the interests of the body, to its health & safety. Emotions are the 'adrenalin' of events, real or imagined.

When they become our complete identity, then we loose touch with our 'heart', the source of our sense of ourselves as sacred & worthy of 'love' & worthy to be 'loved by.' That is the challenge. To properly structure our emotional identity under the absolute authority of our heart & our commitment to that quality of care.

Argumentation & debate... seeking wisdom, not dominance

Today... well, listen to any politician & you get too much argumentation & debate. But little in the way of wisdom being shared... or sought.

Today, everything is used for its potential 'power' to persuade. Including not just argumentation & debate, but all rhetorical behaviors now suffer for the violence of those who deem even communication & ideas should only be theirs to advance, demanding filial piety to & for anti-social values.

If the values we employ to engage life & its occupants requires some form of subservience & subjugation of others, rhetorically & as a matter of seeking wisdom, then such strategies as argumentation & debate merely become another form of oppression & marginalization.

Rights VS love… what we share, not what we keep, in both cases

Rights emerged as an intellectual & political concern because of the nature of the relationships that developed in & over history. Moses, with the emergence of a 'God' who seemed to dictate the nature of the developing relationship, humanity was gifted with an authority that now required, as a part of a new community, to care about others such that we did not bring harm to them.

Because of the need to address such issues, then it is obvious that before, there were harms & stresses to relationships not congruent to community, especially beloved community. This established that people were now 'authorized' towards a civil expectation not the norm before, purely dependent upon the social education & graces of the actors themselves.

It becomes more than a casual incident or chance meeting then, if God exists, in the initial choice of Abraham. The Bible offers that Abraham was considered a man of his word, a man of honor, by choice, in a world where such choices were neither encouraged nor the law of mind or heart. Relationships mattered.

But the 1st right established by God?

That God be given a particular 'space' in the relationship, of a superior nature. It will only be revealed later, with a succession of behaviors, that the real nature of the relationship is revealed.

The 1st right God demands of human, it the right to be their parent.

Hence, if humanity wants to imagine the purposes for which is natural to demand a quality of particular relationship, asserting a 'right', is when it serves more than self-interest, but is actually a benefit to be shared, both now & in the future, as a normative expression of consideration given relationships... natural now to what it means 'to be human'.

God, or its proxy, history, introduced 'rights' as a proper means to a proper social end... always community. The greatest, the 1st right, the ONLY true 'right'? The right to love & its corresponding fruit, the right to be loved.

The 3 Great Blessings... grasping the 'greater' view

Offered in The Bible, is a offering of 'God's will for humanity. Some religious people rightly imagine this as 'blessings' & if we approach life either with that defining echo or we simply listen to the 'cosmos' own rendition of life's greater purposes, we still end up, at either door, with the same prize.

Each other & the choice of how to integrate those two individual & unique social factors.

The 1st blessing is a self-realization of maturing in both the nature of the values chosen to live by, but also in the heart of discipline brought to bear to sustain such commitment. Through all the seasons of life & living. The final fruit realized in the quality of integration offered in morally significant, sustainable relationships.

The 2nd blessing is the emphasis then on the application of that living witness to all the opportunities of life, including & especially as we embrace the role of the 'teachers' of the sacred values of life. This is most critical to the priming of the next generation, hence, the formation of stable parenting 'couples', dedicated to establishing the

95

quality of personal & intimate integration required so as to realize & maximize the social & psychological/spiritual environment most conducive to children's own maturing & developing individuality. This creates the 1st society.

The 3rd blessing is the emphasis then on extending then that individual social system to the totality of environments we are exposed to & integrate with. Especially notable will be the parenting of children as the perfection of our stewardship with the creation. We then become cosmic stewards of the creation, as also the means to sustain our own futures, as individuals & as a species.

In all three 'expectations' is both an expectation of standards for informing the values employed, they all without exception, force to our consciousness the importance of integration, community, will & heart.

It is all about relationships.

The nature of them, the values informing them, the consequences occurring from them.

It is about life & living in it, as a part of it.

Communication… here is needed a 'theology' of integrative communication, for building bridges between social actors & thus intrinsically supporting a natural path to peace

Communication initially is a totally self-centered enterprise, in all environments, under all circumstances. But the purpose for which it is engaged & the form it takes clearly defines the morality of that effort. Ultimately, in each moment of communication is revelation & creation. Revelation of self, our motives fully owned publicly or not. The creation we offer for the other to respond to, to offer equally to. Creation that affirms & sustains community or exploits & potentially harms the environment & its shared actors.

In the end, communication is about community. As its value.

Chapter 4- The 3 Great Human Virtues: The universal global lineage in the search for human friendly 'values' as principles for living

"The new expression of truth should be able to reveal the Heart of God... the broken heart he felt when humankind, his children whom he could not abandon, rebelled against him...& his heart of striving to save them throughout the long course of history." Rev. Sun Myung Moon's Exposition of the Divine Principle

"You must not hate your brother in your heart... You must not take vengeance or bear a grudge against the children of your people, but you must love your neighbor as yourself. I am the Lord." Leviticus 19:17-18

"The key to creating a better & more peaceful world is the development of love & compassion for others." Dalai Lama

"Surely it is permissible *to insert* speculations in the *progression* of a history in order to fill out the gaps in the reports, because what comes before as distant cause, & what follows, as effect, can give a fairly reliable clue for discovering the intervening causes as to make the transition comprehensible." Immanuel Kant

"The rebel... demands a certain degree of freedom for himself; but in no case, if he is consistent, does he demand the right to destroy the existence & the freedom of others. He humiliates no one. The freedom he claims, he claims for all; the freedom he refuses, he forbids everyone to enjoy. He is not only the slave against master, but also man against the world of slave & master. Therefore, thanks to rebellion, there is something more in history than the relation between mastery & servitude." Albert Camus

"History in its pure form furnishes no value by itself." Albert Camus

"The whole of the Torah is for the purpose of promoting peace." Judaism, Talmud, Gittin 59b

"You do not do evil to those who do evil to you, but you deal with them with forgiveness & kindness." The Prophet Mohammad

"Where there is forgiveness, there is God Himself."
Sikhism

"To love is to know me, my innermost nature, the truth that I am." Hinduism

"Allah is all forgiving & loves the one who forgives others." Qur'an 64.14

"All... are created equal". The Constitution of the United States of America

"The true patriot joins with every parent in the nation in the protection & articulation of the value of their own children. The true patriot carries this responsibility not as a burden, but as a joy for the value it creates, the community it realizes." The Last Spiritual Samurai

Intro to the 'values'

The Fearful & Tearful Tango: The historic need for the dance of repentance & forgiveness

Synopsis: The world, from humanity to the creation is suffering the results of unhealthy & unsustainable relationships. We cannot go back in time to restore such effects. The future can only be protected if we can find a way now to embrace the opportunities to change the nature of damaged relationships. Forgiveness, a strategy that is much overlooked for its integrative social value, still alone cannot restore a relationship ravaged by human will. Nor can repentance alone; an even more rare relic of human intercourse healing strategies, repentance cannot heal the recalcitrant heart. In this case, such a heart has refused to embrace the desire for renewal. Important to grasp initially, intuitively or rationally & cognitively, the challenge to restore what has been damaged depends upon conditions of intimacy, vulnerability, commitment to the ideal of love, or merely just a healthy relationship. There will needs be a willingness to let go of the past, to reframe its context & needed attendance, to create a new future, required in how we engage the now. It is on the one hand the most intimate of processes, yet on the other is the engagement of enemies, to whom trust has been broken & is now accepted as a 'natural' state of relationship. Timing, to optimize the opportunity, for both, is critical. The goal? The Tango. The Dance of Love.

Many moral teachers, many philosophers, many of us as parents, many religious leaders & prophets, all of us spoke to the values that would reveal the means to such a perfection of integration.

That is the legacy of humanity, in its care, for itself.

Imagining the 'best practices' values for relationships established a human lineage of defining love, the commitment to relationship, & its supporting cast of repentance & forgiveness, as the common link between all peoples, in all times.

All seeking the perfection that is The Tango… The Dance of Love.

Many people might like to imagine that the sound of one hand clapping produces no sound. But it also might matter what one is 'listening' for, eh?

Another 'romantic' notion is that the use of freedom is about what one does for oneself. That being a 'consumer,' merely & sustainably capitalizing on life's opportunities, is what life is about.

'Reality' is now about 'drama' created for its entertainment value, the more extravagant & indulgent, the better. The more 'emotions' of any kind, the more extreme the temptations to act beyond norms or decency, all have become a form of drug, or status, something you MUST have.

Finally, 'wisdom' today is held to be when one controls some aspect of the pie that others don't or at least control others access to such resources as allows one to be ahead of the game.

In none of the scenarios is integration & community held as a significant value to be entertained as a value either needed nor held in common.

Law is no remedy.

Law is the lazy person's remedy to self-definition & character. If one is lawful in the general way, one is thus 'respectful' & a 'good' citizen. Maybe even a patriot. Or so the fantasy goes.

Don't really give a shit about neighbor nor country, except as it intrudes in one's world in some fashion at least emotionally significant to oneself.

But we live in a world of consequence, intended or not. There used to be enough room for me & my forty acres & a mule, without you intruding on my space. With your mule & forty acres. Now, you might imagine my mule should rightly be yours.

Today, if my mule shits on your forty acres, we may end up in civil court or criminal court, depending how far we take our concerns about our freedom. If you decide you want my mule's shit, we may end up in the same court about who that shit rightfully belongs to.

The sound of one hand clapping begins to sound not so bad, eh?

But is that the solution?

Reality offers us, in its own created witness, the wisdom we need to understand; to both understand our place in the cosmos, & to render a proper judgement on what should prioritize humanity, to become truly human. If we are listening for THAT wisdom, about the personal & social significance of relationships to all humanity, for all time, for all the times of our lives & our living, then our clapping becomes a crescendo of meaning.

That is the gift of life we are born with; the capacity to reason what me must do… & why & by what informing values. Then, as we mature, we understand that our sexual organs are not merely a nice outlet for a winter night, or the source of the next generation, but the secret of life. Within the coupling that we engage in, intelligently or with merely emotional drug highs our intent, life continues in spite of our ignorance.

One molecule inclined now by inbred habits, unites with another. We are well on our way to create the human eye. Movement beyond tolerances previously imagined. Freedom is loosed upon us.

Integration occurs.

A surrendering to possibilities.

Possibilities that always provide more opportunity for 'community' building, opening more doors for opportunity in diversity & complexity of relationships to now 'naturally' develop.

Our bodies, with the physical mind that allows a quality of integration into any environment, even those merely imagined, allows a degree of freedom for both self-creation & self-expression beyond imagination… except for the evidence of what we can create.

Hell… or heaven.

A very immature child MUST imagine oneself the center of the universe. Our hell our evidence. Fortunately…

The rational capacity of the mind continues to mature as a physiological reality until the early twenties, in spite of how well we do or don't do in our use of it.

Our instinct, according to both the success of the cosmos in creating life & to human need & real time benefit of the relationships both to create life & to sustain it, needs require that every person is socialized to not only a universal standard of interpersonal civility, but that such civility is a universal norm.

This then argues, in these times, two important points.

First, is the need & value of such an informed electorate in every nation, that as we act to create families, even our children are subjected to the same quality & universal standard of social civility & community formation & health.

Simply stated, we need to recognize the value of a universal standard of true family values, that based upon human need & potential, can offer all humanity the same hope of both offering children to the future, prepared for that future, but now a future for all such children, not just ours.

This concern must be as well-spread as a form of self-educated environmental concern, not just equal to climate change, but far surpassing it in the need for human action.

Climate change, like criminality, of a legalized version or not, like all social deviance & its effects, is a reflection of the interpersonal values we have allocated our conscience, to remind us of the moral significance of socially embraced opportunities. The conscience a structured system of values that also define the limits of freedom we allow ourselves. But only in environmentally friendly ways if our value orientation embraces our neighbor as equal to oneself.

We continue to imagine freedom like an undisciplined child allowed into a candy store. Each according to how they were raised, & then honoring that raising in the social behaviors offered others. Now, in how & why we engage one another... or not.

Today, social morality reflects children not only out of control, but willfully so, prideful in the rebellion, arguing falsely that the country protects such behavior as a natural right. That is the 1st con.

Anarchy is born.

Freedom is destroyed.

Hell is created.

But... as I surrender to reality, I do not find limits as much as I rediscover my own potential. Life argues its own value. In the living witness of it.

Even in suicide, we do not seek to escape life.

Having no rational means to process our suffering, we seek to end the pain, if not the source.

The suicide at least has the grace not to take revenge on others. To force their enemy to change, or to force their ability to inflict harm on others to cease.

Karl Marx suffered for the world he saw.

Few will ever appreciate how much he suffered.

But he had no solutions, none having been offered him.

He saw the right & wrong of our freedom.

He saw how little we cared about life… or living. Whom truly cares about life... & living, honors all life, as it is living.

But they would not listen, they did not care…

Most would have given up then… but not Marx.

But what he did create, as the ultimate enemy?

In the end, all can be enslaved.

An idea will justify it… just as ideas justified the evil he now sought to destroy.

In the end?

Over 200 million dead people in less than a century.

Billions in slavery now, under governments with no heart, nor the mind of a good parent.

THAT is the wisdom of hate.

THAT is the 'Zen' of hate.

What one truly seeks, one will discover. If one offers oneself to it fully. Good… or evil.

The cosmos offers its own witness to wisdom.

In the meantime…

Create something better than the human body, & in doing so liberate the cosmos to secure its fullest freedom… the living cosmic witness.

In the meantime, wisdom is available.

Wisdom is rational.

Wisdom is accessible.

Wisdom ONLY available to humanity.

… & the freedom needed to act, with wisdom.

A hand offers peace…

Chapter 5- Developing for 2000 years... 'The Tree of Life': "Be ye therefore perfect as..."

"Surely it is permissible to insert speculations in the progression of a history in order to fill out the gaps in the reports, because what comes before as distant cause, & what follows, as effect, can give a fairly reliable clue for discovering the intervening causes as to make the transition comprehensible." Immanuel Kant

"I refuse to accept the idea that the 'isness' of man's present nature makes him morally incapable of reaching up for the eternal 'oughtness' that forever confronts him." Rev. Martin Luther King, Jr.

"Our Master said, "Supposing that it could not be practiced, it seems hard to go on likewise to condemn it. But how can it be good, & yet incapable of being put into practice?" Mo Tzu

"There is the principle of loving all, to take the place of that which make distinctions." Mo Tzu

"Singularity: a point at which a function takes an infinite value, especially in space-time."

"History reveals two qualities of rebels. Those that seek to be a benefit to the world, including their own enemy, in their offering... & those who seek to re-imagine the world, without their enemy, as the result of assuming the right to eliminate the enemy, rather than to integrate with the enemy. This the true contrast between hate & integration... as an act of community building & social & historical restoration." The Last Spiritual Samurai

"The established religions & their adherents have never realized that man has a central responsibility for turning this evil world around." Rev. Sun Myung Moon

"I believe that unarmed truth & unconditional love will have the final word in reality." Rev. Martin Luther King, Jr

"There is no greater love than a man lay down his life for another." Jesus

"Did not Moses give you the law, & yet none of you keepth the law? Why go ye about to kill me?" Jesus

"Be ye therefore perfect as your parent in heaven." Jesus

"No (wo)man is worth his/her salt who is not ready at all times to risk his/her body... to risk his/her well-being... to risk his/her life... in a great cause." Theodore Roosevelt

"All interpretation of meaning, like all scientific observation, strives for clarity & verifiable accuracy of insight & comprehension. The basis for certainty in understanding can either be rational, which can be further subdivided into logical & mathematical, or it can be of an emotionally empathic & artistically appreciative quality... The highest degree of rational understanding is attained in cases involving the meanings of logically or mathematically related propositions; their meaning may be immediately & unambiguously intelligible." Max Weber

I have recently experienced an enhanced & increased sense of knowing when someone speaks to me with a 'forked tongue.' There is no other or better way to describe this experience.

In that moment, my 1st challenge to my commitment to love others, even my enemy, is revealed & engaged.

We all experience this to varying degrees, both in our accuracy of interpretation & in its frequency of occurrence in our lives. Criminals & politicians both become masters of perception & deception. They imagine it as expediency. A needed skill set, worthy of respect, if not admiration.

We properly know it as a form of interpersonal 'hate' of others, that allows one to circumvent moral &

ethical norms or even considerations in the greater service to oneself. Hate merely being the varying degrees of emotionally significant anti-social motives we reveal in our behavior. In this quality of social process, words are used like weapons, both seen & not, implied & used.

Thus, one whom would seek to advantage themselves, by disadvantaging others, is best served to know that person, as well as one might, under such circumstances that such behavior is entertained.

The 'art' of disadvantaging others can be merely situational or it can be a career form of personal investment in mastering certain qualities of skill sets. From the pickpocket to the career politician, both depend upon manipulating a known quantity, as much as needed, for that needed duration. Whether such manipulated parties are aware or not.

Always involved in such skills is the art of listening. To hear what is not said, or said but not owned. But the true masters listen to one above all others. Themselves.

It does not mean they are honest, moral, caring or exhibit any other social skill of integration & community. They own all the little games, lies, self-deceptions, manipulation techniques they played on themselves, to reach such a moral plateau that the normal parameters of a social conscience is not only denied, but redesigned to exploit ANYTHING others might offer, erringly or not.

Strangely, Jesus, & Moon, by proxy of his own choices & use of freedom, both employed the same skill set. Know thyself, that one might then master creating the final masterpiece. But, if one seeks such knowledge, to use that self for a greater good, to serve to others what they need most, then that knowledge of others does not disadvantage one nor does it seek profit.

With such personal insight, both Jesus & Moon understand perfectly what such self-application reveals & realizes in oneself.

As they then encountered others, they merely saw & encountered a variation of their own life processes & choices & opportunities. Once I no longer lie to myself, not out of arrogance, but for the lack of true offering we can then make to others, it is much easier to observe the same processes in others, including when they think we are NOT aware.

It forced Jesus & Moon to the same cliff edge... push the people off & let them live with the consequences of their misuse of freedom, the missed opportunities for the quality of relationship that even God can share in, naturally.

Or... recognize the need, act to relieve it, & thus, serve the people in the ONLY way to produce the fruits all want, all need, yet none have committed to co-creating.

Jesus & Moon thus offered to 'know' every man & every woman, not intimately in a personal way, but intimately in the way we enter another's life when we offer them words whose effect can be of moral significance & thus, impact & alter their behavior.

We share then in the fruits of such effort, of such investment. When we act to aid another, the benefit that they realize in their own effort, is part of the living legacy of our investment in life & living. We act as a form of surrogate parent to their own creative efforts with others.

For the fruits Jesus & Moon sought were not for themselves; as with the same effort, we will pleasantly discover that the fruit we sought for others, offers us not just relief for the opportunity maturely nurtured & natured, but the quality of meaning that life can only return under such circumstances.

The Wheel of Life may seem a nice, esoteric image for children & a feel good moment, but it is actually the reality that we must surrender to, to own our own wisdom.

Jesus dealt with a simple people.

Jesus was a simple person.

Jesus also knew the conflicting hearts of the people.

He most resented those who imagined they were entitled to a quality of privilege & position that did not honor the role they played.

They spoke to God for the people...

God spoke to them for the people...

That role requires a quality of attendance in both directions that elevates the parties to be of one accord, one heart, one mind, one body.

The revelation of Jewish history, as revealing a pattern of moral social evolution, argues a humanity at least in touch enough with itself to seemingly have a sense of moral direction, that addressed human history as a sustained act of bad faith needing correction.

The 'Jewish experience,' an experience born in a forced confrontation with an 'authority' that assumed to be superior to that of humanity, argued for a more nuanced form of relationship to be developed & hence, honored now as a valued tradition. This included the idea that one's offering to one's 'superiors,' as parents, gods or demons, required a degree of attendance & 'heart', or the will to care, that humanity was no longer alone in the universe, but had an entity also concerned about human life & experiences. Humanity now REALLY mattered.

THAT is a revelation to challenge all revelations.

I matter... to God.

BUT... what I thus do, will be of consideration... morally significant to my potential relationship now developing. The 'revealed' God is a god of demands, expectations, standards... like every parent acts.

Hence, also establishing patterns of unconscious, but morally significant behavior, all offering towards community... the relationship. A tradition & pattern of integration that would be experienced as both normal & normative. Suggesting a needed but natural discipline be employed, not as force, but as habit & a naturally affirming experience of health & social & therefore, political stability.

Civilization exists between humanity & its God.

The fabled 'Tree of Life' is understood by many as a symbol of the human realization of God's will, for humanity. This indicating the quality of values informing the relationship are such that 'children' of God emerge, mature in the sense of a full integration of the values of God is effected, thus securing self & all others as always significant to the moment & what we thus offer.

The Tree of Life is the mature expression of individuality as it seeks & integrates into community. Be this integration for a moment or for a lifetime. The Tree of Life is the heart measure of the human use of freedom, coupled with will & the educated & embraced desire for a certain quality of relationship, as a sustainable life living choice.

With Moses, God further revealed the sanctity & sacredness of the relationship with God, that God sought. But for humanity, with humanity, not just God. Loving God with all one's heart & being, if that requires I also NOT harm my neighbor, then establishes a new priority for the relationships God cares about.

It seems, both me & my neighbor not only matter to God, but should matter to each of us, singly, but also as a consummated community, established by God. A community ALL in covenant. Yet, if in covenant with God, each & every person, then each & every one now is also consummated to each other.

The evolution of a programmed socialization, developing a sense of self that MUST include others, not just God, exactly the same challenge EVERY parent faces in preparing their children for the future, when the quality of effected integration will also determine the quality of its fruit, as a human creation of heart, will & values, argued the Jewish experience became the human portal experience that we all must process to realize community... be it a family, nation or marriage.

Parenting, the encouragement towards a quality of moral self-realization, embracing a transformation emerging from an expanding self-definition to include others, finalized in the role of parenting, allows a degree of self-transcendence not realizable any other way. It is a quality of the use of freedom that while engaged unconsciously for the most part, insures we are most prepared for the challenges ahead.

Why?

Whom has the heart of God towards all life, then acts as God would act. The freedom to choose to love, to care, to integrate, is never denied those who seek to be human, a child of God. That others may not choose to engage that freedom is always the option God provided, but could not control.

Yet, in response to human potential & human need, from birth to death, for its capacity to create sustainable community, even in the most hostile of environments, freedom to choose the values we engage, to define ourselves, argues we seek that wisdom that age & experience might support, but which we need to cognitively define for ourselves.

Throughout history, as the result of social moral evolution or of God re-priming humanity, Jewish history & other singular figures sought a path forward where reason could justify NOT harming others, even if we could not yet rationally justify 'love'.

Today, in understanding the ONLY & natural purpose love & relationships can serve, the wisdom of ages is now accessible to the least, no less than any who imagine some entitlement to social advantage.

Yet, the beauty of it all is that The True Family Values allow ONLY a shared profit to emerge, in any community, as a result of any kind of effort. The evolution of moral consideration that must be given to life & living, ONLY takes on true political significance when it is the shared paradigm to define all relationships. The very purpose & value of True Family Values is as obvious as capitalism. One seeks the opportunity for the self, to serve the self, by serving the whole community... the other seeks to use the community, for serving only the self, or the self as the prime intended benefactor.

While the true value & values defined & defended within Jewish history are not yet understood for the universal value they offer to the conversation on the meaning of 'being human,' they still offer a pattern that optimizes the opportunity for a socialization to a mindset that discovers one's greatest value is realized in relationship. This also the venue for such creative expression that individuality is never an issue of community & integration.

If & when we grasp the global & sociological moral significance of the social development that is Jewish history, we discover ourselves. We discover we are really looking at a mirror... the distinction being in the specific use of will & freedom, not the quality of values informing the consequent behaviors.

Jew, Muslim, atheist, Hindu, American, Russian, Communist & capitalist, all in the end employ the values that define the true love family. To some degree, to undeterminable impact.

Every parent is a parent if they do more than merely provide material necessities for children. If they also

115

imagine they need a moral central point to define self, & self to all others. The challenge & problems only emerge in the standard known & applied.

Hence, though all may not truly know Jesus at all, for the revolutionary understanding of the values needed for true human consumption, to be children of God or the cosmos, all cultures & all peoples understood the social significance of commitment to care, forgiveness & repentance, as restorational behaviors as much as human defining. The conclusion then that wisdom has been around for a long time.

But the concluding insight?

ONLY offered in The True Family Values, as part of the process of defining oneself & how one will view the rest of the world, as an opportunity for significant integration, forgiveness & repentance becomes central to EVERYTHING we must imagine we may need in a world not yet convinced love is such a great solution. ONLY The True Family Values honors the challenges posed by life & by the need to parent children who can integrate naturally into community such that the only rational remedy, to protect all, is secured as a matter of maturity, the recognition of value beyond self.

Jewish history established the pattern.

Perfection, the revelation of the child of God, is merely the mature individual who has integrated the ONLY values needed to both define & secure both the individual & the community it shares, in such form as to establish true peace & security.

The True Family Values... revealing The Tree of Life.

The Talmud fulfilled.

The covenant now not just a potential, but a realizable reality.

Jesus offering the concluding but defining piece of the puzzle... love requires a habit of caring that takes one

116

beyond the horizon of harm that is the current state of humanity & their relationships. We must consent to aid our enemy, to return to community. To return to life.

Jesus marked the final bridge that must be crossed.

The enemy waits on one side. We, on the other.

Jesus encourages us forward... until integration occurs.

The living statement then of both.

6000 years... we are almost home.

Freedom, to choose, the last fork in the road.

How will I define you... to me.

Chapter 6-- "Getting to know you, getting to know all about you...": The 'madness' of loving one's enemy

"...just as Jesus willingly gave his life so that the world might live, God wanted all Christians to be willing to give themselves for the salvation of the world. However, today, Christians of the world are not even close to realizing this heart of God." Rev. Sun Myung Moon

"When the individual & the families which transcend racial & national barriers gather together to create a church, a society & nation, that nation will become God's ideal nation for all peoples." Rev. Sun Myung Moon

"If you allow God to leave America... this nation will decline; it will be subjugated by satanic hands. When this happens, America will be dismal, America will become a living hell." Rev. Sun Myung Moon

"Today we are living in the age WHEN WE MUST LOOK AT EVERY INDIVIDUAL & EVERY

NATION AS VITAL COMPONENTS OF THE WORLD..." Rev. Sun Myung Moon

"The love of forgiveness is the contextual application of the original desire for relationship, now applied to a situation in which a common community is NOT the co-creation effected, but a relationship in which harm was. Forgiveness is the affirmation that "I am still here for you... as I always was." The Last Spiritual Samurai

"Oneself, indeed, is one's savior, for what other savior could there be? With oneself well controlled one obtains a savior difficult to find." Buddhism

Who dares imagines themselves as 'unlovable'? Who can shoulder such a burden of heart? What form of relief would we need to seek, should we seek, to gain such wisdom as needed for such a confrontation?

Even more bold, even more daring, who imagines themselves so in need of morally significant social evolution, that they would make any offering, however sacred the offering, make any promise, if only we might be/do/feel differently than we have done/do/will do?

Jesus, in his encounter with God, experienced the deep despair that is human experience. He knew the shame of being human. He knew the heartache of longing, that not only that life could be & should be different, but that it should first reveal itself in the hearts of those most suffering, most lost without hope, without vision, dream or even the smallest of experience of beloved community.

Yet, unlike so many of us, Jesus' experience of shame led to desire for others, not just himself, his situation. He knew that intimately. But he also could look around.

He saw the disparity of wealth between the haves & have nots. He saw this wealth as it was, an unearned spiritual sense of wealth, determined by the 'evidence' of physical wealth or control of those with such wealth. Jesus realized that the poor in spirit, were in that state as a result of the quality of relationships that had been determined their lot. Determined by the length & breadth of social response & affirmation that leads one to still believe in God, but to assume one is not important to God's immediate or providential purposes.

The poor, so often then also led to be poor in spirit, learns first-hand the meaning of 'not mattering.' Even though the whole of Jewish history was now positioned to honoring a particular relationship, in particular ways, the benefit of which held to be in some kind of trust, such insight not immediately available for understanding; this for some reason humanity was not privy to & to which God was admirably silent… that imagined benefit receding in our hearts if the living were too challenging.

A promise of benefit to relationship cannot always carry us through the hard times, the dark times. This left many Jews praying for God's intercession, but never understanding how & why God MIGHT act. Or what God might ask of humanity next.

Moses' revelation of God's heart of concern for the quality of relationships humanity was entertaining itself with, should & could have worked as a true spiritual awakening. Where no one had been no more compelled to care about another than one was emotionally & experientially inclined to, with Moses' '10 words', humanity was informed that not only did we matter to God, but our attendance to one another should also now naturally include all those around me, to whom I have access to.

Humanity mattered. Hence, from a moral point of view...

Human relationships should embrace that potential.

Yet, Jesus' rational assessment of Jewish history, coupled with his own experiences & observations, led to particular conclusions. The words of Moses, while actually complete unto themselves, to inform the people as to the values that naturally produce The True Family Values, did not inspire both the needed moral readjustment, both individually as well as collectively, that would have so informed the people in the living of their lives, that Jesus' words of reconciliation with God, requiring a corresponding reconciliation with one another, should have been the social state shared by all who imagined & called themselves 'Jews'.

Instead, Jesus entered a world not only to be served by the 'messiah' in the completeness of God's word, now to be shared as normative for all people, but a world that had devolved to the point that the living expression & social/civil evolution that should have naturally occurred, instead revealed a people much fragmented, in their understanding of God & in their expectations of themselves, in relationship to God & neighbor.

When conceptually considered or allowed its natural interpretation, Jewish history offers that the Jews had come to be 'socialized' to a moral expectation both of God & of themselves.

121

If one truly loves God with all one's heart, mind & soul, then one naturally would NEVER even imagine taking from another, lying to another, giving false witness against another. If God loves me, but states I need love you, by not harming you, then in doing so, I am loving you also. If God loves you, & I love you, God will know that & thus, in God's eyes, my faith is complete.

In the revelation of the '10 words', humanity was informed that not only were we to care about God, but now we were to extend that care to all... parents, children, neighbor... enemy.

Yet, Jews allowed wisdom from God to become an external force to impose that will for human interpersonal relationships, instead forming into an institution that punishes 'anarchy' or rebellion or failures to comply.

NOT THE KIND OF RELATIONSHIPS GOD SOUGHT...

Where God sought such education that the human heart, the choice to will to love, would be encouraged, enhanced & elevated as a social 'good', hence forcing the issue of the use of freedom to be a high value aspect of our reasoning, laws removed the responsibility to the 'parent' for a continued encouragement towards beloved community. This became a form of law with a punitive element to it.

Including the death penalty.

Jesus knew that a God whom had created life, would not willingly destroy that life. Even if it 'sinned'. Jesus spoke to two such issues when confronted by the men with the woman 'caught' in adultery. A woman obviously not loving God with all her heart, mind & soul.

Human laws demanded her death.

Those confronting Jesus sought to use her against Jesus. THAT was a sin to create harm.

Hence, in their hearts, they gave false witness to God of their intent, their values & their heart of attendance to God, in engaging God's other children.

Jesus could see all of this.

The woman, Jesus chastised, advising her to sin no more. Her repentance now less an issue than those who stood to accuse her, to hurt Jesus.

Jesus knew she needed & would be directly benefitted by the forgiveness that shares the shame of her bad behavior, while sharing with her the means to restore it. Accept my sin, by repenting it, by changing the person who created the sin, that I sin no more.

Jesus knew nothing more about that woman than that she was a pawn in a larger 'game', but one who was charged with a 'serious' breach of relationship, one critical to the health of not only those directly involved, but also affecting children, family & friends.

Yet, Jesus knew what each relationship needed, to offer the love situationally relevant to the events emerging with him. The woman received the kind of forgiveness that acknowledges she herself is not seeking to repent, her shame not only public, but she also now seeking freedom, as is suggested in her response to Jesus. Accepting his judgment & his restorational path for her.

Those who sought to accuse Jesus, by accusing the woman, Jesus forgave in the ONLY way meaningful to their needs & their state of 'sin'. He challenged their motives & their heart values. He offered that they themselves were the 'sinners' in such agendas, not revealing God in themselves, nor seeking to establish God between them, as a shared experience. Jesus' judgment of events allowed all to accept the 'truth' & then, dependent upon the heart of response, to defend or to repent, would now be the measure of their quality of rational use of freedom & the human will to be.

Judgement accepted… repentance & community established. Restoration of heart realized, healed.

Accusation accepted… self-defense & an adversarial relationship exists on all sides. Anarchy is defended.

Jesus could 'see' all of this, Jesus could then choose how to respond to this… but it would be his chosen values, lived, that would reveal his heart of attendance, offered. People could come as enemies to him, but the door to relationship was still open, but ONLY when the values chosen inform us that the person in front of us matters, no matter what, that we then must act with human wisdom. A wisdom that acknowledges that all matter, always, even when deviant & sinners.

Hence, Jesus, to love others who sought to harm him, was 'forced' by the circumstances to alter the nature of the desired form of offering to create community, to one that could ONLY offer such response as to redirect the relationship to one of acknowledgment of a breakdown, now needing community involvement to restore it.

Jesus did not seek to shut doors to the potential for relationship, but rather to own that the relationship needed to be of a particular quality of informing moral & ethical considerations.

Jesus thus realized that such an educational effort was very much in the nature of the challenge children must face as they evolve as morally responsible social agents. This requires we also repent for when we are 'sinning', that in doing so, we restore ourselves to ourselves as loving, restore ourselves to community as loving. This heals us no less than those we have harmed, who now seek to share in the process of forgiveness & community restoration.

Jesus thus offered both a living witness to the need for love of enemy, such that we 'know' how to respond to them, but he also illustrated its public use. Sometimes it will be as with children. Then we share the process of restoration, acting as a source of moral encouragement & support. We sustain community in this effort, towards the day when community is fully re-established.

Jesus' emphasis on love of enemy, forgiveness & repentance, offers he understood that while Jewish law was complete, the people's understanding & commitment to its purpose & original value was now lost &/or hidden.

The Jewish leaders, nominally also to represent God's interest in the people & to the people, was now so far off course as to suggest the leaders were favored by God over the rest of the people.

Jesus knew the leadership, in their misrepresentations of God, in their behavior & informing values, were NOT representing God or God's interests in the people, now to be understood as in a familial relationship. One naturally embracing a quality of intimacy & vulnerability we imagine we wanted with our own physical parents, even if it did not happen.

As the protectors of the faith of the people, such leadership, as has happened all throughout human history, many became more interested in their positions as status & due entitlements than in the service their positions were created for.

Jesus' anger & resentment would be natural to one who imagines God as parent, but with one always, in every moment, hence also when others shame that God in their own behaviors. Such shaming then removing such people AS representatives to & for the people, for God.

Jesus could only call them back to their own original commitments, this to be their repentance, their indemnity condition needed to restore themselves, to God & to community betrayed.

In this, Jesus loved those who had betrayed God & man. Jesus' forgiveness a contextual offering made to adult children, not kids. Hence, needing the kind of chastisement that acknowledges they knew better, yet continued on course to alienate God in their lives.

If this were the state of the leaders, & with a little reading of the history of the times of Jesus makes it abundantly clear that the concerns that had prompted God to speak to Moses, were now in full retreat, then we know the average people suffered such moral deprivation no less themselves.

This marks it why Jesus emphasized that those who would be God's children, lived as God's children would live, with each other.

Jesus offered that repentance, love of enemy & forgiveness, were the values of the children of God. These values led to the peacemakers. Those who might know who were 'more' guilty, but rather would seek for restoration, healing, & re-establishment of beloved community.

In every public confrontation Jesus was led & challenged to defend himself. Instead, he defended values he knew all needed, knew they knew they needed, but were not in such a society that such values were its civil norm.

Hence, every public confrontation was between enemies, established as such by those seeking Jesus, but not relationship with Jesus. Individuals needing to defend themselves… from the values they were supposedly wedded to.

Jesus' rhetorical confrontations were, judging from his efforts, to be informative & liberating. Even though the events orchestrated by others were also intended to portray & betray Jesus as some deviant.

So Jesus offers history the witness of a true child of God, interfacing with a leadership not morally accountable for its own deviances. Jesus offers what a parent must do with adult children, to try to encourage a moral commitment that has at least waned, if it were ever truly in evidence.

Jesus offers that the daily grind of the office of the messiah is no less tempered by constant confrontation with the needs of people, BUT PEOPLE NOT DESIRING TO CHANGE, FOR ANY REASON.

Jesus' resultant behavior then the evidence of the heart of a parent, forced to attend rebellious children, more suited to anarchy & social terrorism than to beloved community, the very community that all the pain & misery speaks to as a needed relief.

Jesus KNEW the people.

Jesus KNEW God.

Jesus had one choice…

Accept & then act.

Jesus did.

He created The True Family Values.

As not only rhetoric, but Jesus offered it as a living witness, in living color.

You want to touch that Jesus of history?

Inherit his love.

Then turn around.

Chapter 7: Against the grain: Our anti-social personality as deviant

"The core of any effort to teach is to 'raise the question...'"

"The purpose of this essay is once again to face the reality of the present, which is logical crime, & to examine meticulously the arguments by which it is justified; it is an attempt to understand the times in which we live." Albert Camus

"Only a refusal to hate or kill can put an end to the chain of violence in the world & lead us toward a community where men can live together without fear. Our goal is to create beloved community & this will require a qualitative change in our souls as well as a qualitative change in our lives." Rev. Martin Luther King, Jr.

"A man is a true Muslim when no other Muslim has to fear anything from either his tongue or his hand." Islam: Hadith of Bukhari

"Not one of you is a believer until he loves for his brother what he loves for himself." Islam, Forty Hadith of an-Nawawi 13

"All God really desires for each of us is to discover the joy of truly engaging others fully, when we seek to truly love them... it's that simple." The Last Spiritual Samurai

"The passage from the state of nature to the civil state produces in man a very remarkable change, by substituting in his conduct justice for instinct, & by giving his actions the moral quality that they previously lacked. It is only when the voice of duty succeeds physical impulse, & the law succeeds appetite, that man, who till then had only regarded himself, see that he is obliged to act on other principles, & to consult his reason before listening to his inclinations." Jean-Jacques Rousseau

Social scientists have now united with religious moral criticism of the human use of will & freedom. The resulting paradigm actually nails the most self-centered interpersonal, anti-social behaviors, revealing the underlying, informing, morally significant values that create any anti-social public posture & anti-integrative efforts.

That social scientists have identified what they call the 'dark side' of human behaviors is only to finally admit that there is a form of deviance that MUST be acknowledged as against both the individual, & collective interests of humanity, in equal significance. In this, these social scientists have offered a universal tool & means to both identify 'sin' & also to clearly identify that anti-social elements, values & behaviors ARE against the public interests, of any nation. As is indicated in the nature of the personal & social impact upon the individual, the ecological system they are a part of, hence, the environment & its communities.

For clarity, here is the reasoned 'science' of social criticism, both needed & illuminated to & for the sake of all of us; for we will recognize ourselves, at times & places we might now wish to forget... or better, now restore.

Egoism: The excessive concern with one's own pleasure or advantage at the expense of community well-being.

Machiavellianism: Manipulativeness, callous affect, and strategic-calculating orientation.

Moral Disengagement: A generalized cognitive moral orientation to the world that differentiates individuals' thinking in a way that powerfully affects unethical behavior.

Narcissism: An all-consuming motive for ego-reinforcement.

Psychological Entitlement: A stable and pervasive sense that one deserves more and is entitled to more than others.

Psychopathy: Deficits in affect, callousness, self-control, and impulsivity.

Sadism: Intentionally inflicting physical, sexual, or psychological pain or suffering on others in order to assert power and dominance or for pleasure and enjoyment.

Self-Interest: The pursuit of gains in socially valued domains, including material goods, social status, recognition, academic or occupational achievement, and happiness.

Spitefulness: A preference that would harm another but that would also entail harm to oneself. This harm could be social, financial, physical, or an inconvenience.

Such a recognition, by our social scientists, that there is an anti-social side to the use of human freedom, that is problematic for humanity, as individuals & as nation states, even as families, MUST be acknowledged... for the challenge & harms it creates, for all of us, for all human history.

Such anti-social values embrace & define the ultimate values of capitalism.

Such a social paradigm is at the heart of EVERY capitalist.

It is also shared by communists, racists, white nationalists, sexists, & of course, our environmental exploiters.

Remember the verse, "how often I have longed to gather the children..."? That, coupled with the idea of we should consider 'doing onto others as...", in those simple words, seldom have I uncovered a more misunderstood minor, but major 'truth' than in those two.

First, Jesus reveals the heart of EVERY parent in that lament, who has suffered as their children suffered, yet no remedy was possible, for the willfulness of the 'beast' itself. Then, as Jews all understood, because of the need for both the original '10 words' of God, & the subsequent ill-advised hundreds of laws the Jews harnessed themselves,

131

we need the constant reminder of our 'obligation.' To each other. For our own sake.

But actually, in the long & short of it, an obligation to whom? Our 2nd selves. The very image of why I must be considered a sacred form of life & accorded such treatment. In concert with all other such entities.

Jesus' admonition to a public mind towards others, was also teaching us the value of ourselves, as 'we' should be engaged & integrated with. In such value acts, we defend our own value as being absolute, hence, an absolute offering.

Our parents teach us to value ourselves when they guide us away from anti-social, anarchical behaviors. They guide us towards the social reality of the necessity & value of relationships of a particular moral quality.

This socialization occurs as both a cognitive proactive confrontation & education, as well as the natural education that emerges from experience.

As little children, our first form of offered love was obedience, the first form of 'faith' all humanity experiences. This the measure of our now developing maturity, that potential will & capacity for integration we all share, as a sustained moral state, with others. The social significance of such experience is life altering. It will open doors to new ways of being or seal avenues of opportunity away, not from view, but from access.

The abused & unloved child NEVER matures, obedience a sentence to suffering, not love of self or others. Hence, if obedience only promises the bitter fruit of hate & harm, then rebellion speaks for its suffering.

If there is no means to understand how to process abuse & suffering as a child, anger & rebellion are the ONLY immediately viable means to express the state one is in, the challenge not yet even understood, hence, no intelligible communication is rationally possible, or even accessible. The child thus appears 'mad,' as in psychologically unstable & pathologically threatened.

We learn to love ourselves in various ways.

Importantly, we learn this by honoring others as we would be honored. This first socialization of children to community is most easily achieved in a family with more than one child.

The eldest child may be the most challenged, since they naturally act as an aid to socializing their siblings with their own behavior, as siblings, as opposed to the experience of ONLY raised initially by vertical authority figures.

The eldest child is thus always under judgement, no 'safe' harbor but oneself to go to in times of struggle. UNLESS THE PARENTS OFFER SUCH SUPPORT THAT SUCH PROTECTED VULNERABILITY IS SUSTAINED, IN THE DARKEST OF MOMENTS, AS IN THE NOONDAY SUN.

Then, the challenge of the aloneness of maturing is mitigated & the process not lightened, but enlightened.

As we are socialized from every avenue of experience as to the inevitability & potential value of relationships, & thus people, we discover in the process our own moral justifications for integration & community. We come to 'own' our space by the quality of offering we make towards others naturally.

We establish an authority about ourselves, the moral statement as to the value we offer towards the needs & value of integration & community. Our staggered & often uneven maturing process, with a corresponding nurtured & natured desire, develops into habits. But more to the point, we define our own nature, in the context of what it means & must mean, 'to be human.'

If to love another is to invest oneself fully in the opportunity before oneself, for a moment or a lifetime, as a morally significant effort at integration, then to serve oneself so as to insure one's own success in community relationships, is then to offer oneself love of the highest order.

As this becomes habit, it becomes not our 2nd nature, but our true nature.

In this, as a 'good' parent, we, with our parents & all others, 'raised' ourselves to be 'the people of the word.'

The challenge for us today, is that we do not start at point '0'. Because of human history, there are no 'true parents' who have taught us all how to live with one another. We have all had to accept what was our lot in life, with whatever passed for traditions of parenting.

For children abused & confused by life, their future is an unintentional life of deviance & social maladjustment. Of course, our fault.

If we are not truly loved by our parents, then we are bereft the resources, the paradigm & example needed to alter our circumstances, meaningfully. If we find no social resource to supplement that loss of experience & insight, then we wander the halls of deviance & harm, not as a matter of choice, but of having no recognizable alternatives or options.

We become the 'problem' for others, who have no clue, never having experienced such deprivation.

The man who fasts cannot understand the hunger of those forced to fast.

The man who rides atop the elephant cannot understand that even with his elevated viewpoint (re:status), he cannot actually understand either the elephant in its totality nor can he understand the limitations of the understanding he has.

We need all realms of experience, & the right values to encounter & engage them.

To love oneself, if one has been so deprived, also requires some means to such exposure that one can reason what one has not experienced, & by such experience, then

134

begin the process needed to learn that which was not taught, now that one knows the right question.

However we imagine it, loving oneself first requires we not only know & own who we are, as we are, we need then to be willing to invest in that entity ourselves, as both worthy of our effort, but really needing that personal touch that only we give life in our own choices.

Wisdom, before or after, reveals what experience teaches. We choose to care, because we know its value from experience, or we know its value because of the effect of its deprivation has on the quality of life one experiences.

Either educational paradigm works... one creating harm & its attendant environmental impacts that then require restoration, the other the natural education of socialization where we experience our own sacred sense of our value, from the experience of the behaviors of others.

If we start from a negative, the challenge to learn to love oneself becomes not only more haphazard, but we are also prone to social blunders the quality of which could have been avoided with a proper & healthy socialization as a child.

Then we learn how to forgive, ourselves as others, recognizing how forgiveness is actually a very proactive continuation of personal investment. We learn to initiate community, in healthy ways, be it a single person or a nation. We illuminate the heart of integration, in our sincerity & principles of care we offer to others, naturally, the statement of the who, how & what we are with all others.

These are the actions of self-love.

Always in the context of our enjoining others & offering to them the unique experience of our love.

The final hurdle though is one created before birth, that is the legacy of history, that no parent can circumvent, but each must engage, to both restore history, but also to release from the bondage of history, the harms we each offer to the next generation, through the undisciplined emotional content we engage, both psychologically, but also physiologically.

Our final challenge is also from ourselves... how we order our emotional identities in relationship to our conscience, the social contract to care we make with ourselves, as a living guide. This is the final lap of personal & social evolution & moral restoration.

Our emotions are the root of both identity & moral sensibility as a social expression. The first emotional identity is created in the last trimester of experience for the fetus, an identity that is altered in its natural development.

We are born reactionary.

We spend the first years restoring that experience.

But its impact is so subtle & lasting, that we fail to recognize its place & impact in our lives.

In a later chapter, we will focus on this final challenge... the challenge to create a true heart centered conscience, free of the limitations imposed by the past, offering the values to aid as keys even to the freedom of abusive habits.

It is all part of loving oneself.

To offer oneself a quality of freedom few have experienced in life... & living.

By offering it to others, as the statement of who we are, how we are, & what we are, as we engage & integrate with all others.

Understanding the values that lead to anti-social personality tendencies & behaviors, frees us from human history, frees us from our own past & offers us the respite of a view of the future now attainable.

Humanity is a realizable social condition, using current stock. Us.

The choice... to be or not to be... human.

Chapter 8: The secret restorational celebration of life: Repentance as self-love & liberation

"If freedom is to be extended, it must discipline itself both personally & communally. On the personal level this means developing a unity of purpose so that choosing & action are harmonious for the self. This also involves a communal awareness & concern for the individual is part of society. Thus, unity has normative features in conjunction with freedom." John K Roth

"In what sense then is there a human nature, a specific nature that is common to all the species? The answer can be given in a single word: *potentialities*. Human nature that is constituted by all the potentialities that are the species-specific properties common to all the human species.
Man is to a great extent a self-made creature. Given a range of potentialities at birth, he makes of himself what he becomes by how freely he chooses to develop those potentialities by the habits he forms." Mortimer J Adler

Many might be shocked or incredulous that we imagine repentance & self-love as two sides of the same coin.

Even of greater surprise & general consternation occurs when clarity is brought to bear on what we seek when we seek to repent. While the full nature of our effort is yet to be understood, there is a process that we must undergo, naturally, that defines our role & the social significance of our offering. Offering, as opposed to sacrifice.

1st, we suffer the shame of self-realization.

Both of exposure & of the 'fact' of the deviance... further complicated by its impact, personally & environmentally. Hence, the damage that relationships must then suffer, known or not.

If this shame does not devolve to accusation, then our emotional tone & reasoned desire will move us to want to 'fix' the past. To restore that past to as if it had not happened. But we can't do that.

But 'we' can change.

If we can change, then our social impact, our social value, our significance in our efforts at integration, will matter.

We will come to matter in unexpected ways.

If we seek to restore, we can choose to own those values that informed our emotional content, reasoning & subsequent behavior. Owning them by admitting them, their nature & inherit value orientation & then comparing that to both potential of the past & the present, this towards an eye of what we can create, now, for the future, that the past need not be repeated.

As we act in new ways, we discover a sense of release, of fresh air, as if we were on the outside of the walls that imprisoned our hearts. We realize that our deviance affected even our sense of the world around us.

Colors are brighter, lines more defined, opportunities more clear for their potential value. People & things matter...

Then we get the biggest surprise as a cognitive self-given gift.

When we repented, when we sought to restore the relationship, when we offered anything & all that might help, we look back to see who was loved, who might have been aided by our reformation, by our re-integration.

There, at the head of the line, not seeking to be loved 1st, but the one needing 1st aid first, we discover... ourselves.

In our 1st act to restore what was not loved... the cosmos naturally recognized as the source of the problem, it was not the victim. But a source now to be aided, that it might in turn aid, for the value of the experience, both personally & as a public need to be offered in kind, for the wisdom that will inform it.

The great paradox.

Healing humanity requires we love that which declares it needs no love, seeks no love, yet cries for justice.

Justice is 1st realized in the self-love we offer others, of our commitment to love ourselves.

Then WE have acted with justice, & thus, created a just environment.

Until then... under the sentence of deviance, repentance is the key to our freedom, even liberating our neighbor to their own supported opportunity, in the sacred environment we have created for ourselves, now shared as a matter of defending the values of my nation. My neighbor the 1st line of my defense of those values.

Then, any I have harmed. Repentance the means...

Repentance always the way home, if we get lost.

Repentance acting as the shame that offers we still desire community, not isolation & marginalization that are

139

the natural fruits of anarchy & its attendant harms. Repentance the love offering unconsciously but critically laid before oneself first… but to all others then in the effect of restoration.

In the process of engaging our deviance, once we have experienced the initial judgment of our actions, we are always faced with two immediate challenges. Each suggests its direction we must then follow.

First, how we will we emotionally process such an experience? Will we need to defend ourselves, less concerned with the truth as opposed to reality & its attendant but unavoidable social & environmental consequences? Or will our heart lead us to the shame that says what I have created, I would have not. Yet, since I have, what recourse is then available to me, to restore this?

One leads to purgatory. We hear laughter, excitement…

One leads to a judgment hall. There is only silence…

We choose… by what path we then take… towards celebration & excitement… or the silence.

We choose… either, then…

One is held accused, placed center, to satisfy a public, affected directly, collaterally or merely as spectators. The air is almost celebratory, were it not for the intent of the audience. Here then are our enemies, those who would pleasure… in our displeasure. They salute us, they call out to us.

Or…we chose…

The other is more somber.

These appear as judges.

Those 'accused' in purgatory must satisfy others. There is no principle other than defined accusation.

Those appearing in a judgment hall…

They discover others, but whom will seek to aid… caution is suggested, for the price is high.

140

Vulnerability.
Intimacy.
Commitment to care.
Discipline of heart.
Acts… behavioral.
Integration… expressing gratitude.
Freedom.
Restored beloved community.
(Even to 'the man in the mirror.' Then we have met 'forgiveness' in all its potential.)

Chapter 9~ Social integration of the 'divine principle' of the nature of 'God': The Heart & Sacred Role of Parenting

"God's truth is sent to earth as a revelation given through certain providential figures. God's truth is the absolute truth, which is an almighty key capable of solving any problem, no matter how difficult it may be... When this truth is applied to society, social problems can be settled, & when this truth is applied to the world, world problems can be realistically solved... This is a new view of life, a new view of the world, a new view of the universe, & a new view of the providence of history that has never before existed. It is also a principle of integration that can encompass the whole into one unity, while at the same time preserving the individual characteristics of all religious doctrines & philosophies." Rev. Sun Myung Moon

"Let all mankind be thy sect..." Sikhism

"The daily concern of the Parent is the single-heartedly 'how the best I can advance arrangements to save all of you.'" Tenrikyo

"We, today, need... a means to awaken a sense of shame within the oppressor & challenge his false sense of superiority. But the end is reconciliation, the end is redemption, the end is the creation of beloved community... It's love that will bring about miracles in the heart of men." Rev. Martin Luther King, Jr.

"Israel's reconciliation with God can be achieved only when they are all one brotherhood." Judaism, Talmud

"Even a Gentile, if he practices the Torah, is equal to the High Priest." Judaism, Sifra 86b

"...even as citizenship requires civility, so civility points beyond itself to certain permanent & objective moral standards-to the nature of "civil government," &, higher still, to the moral & theoretical concerns of what rightly is called civilization." Charles R Kesler

"The end & aim of wisdom is repentance & good deeds."
Judaism, Talmud

"Repent, for the kingdom of heaven is at hand." Jesus

"Great is repentance; it turns premediated sins into incentives for right conduct." Judaism, Talmud

"Where there is forgiveness, there is God Himself."
Sikhism, Adi Granth, Shalok, Kabir, p 1372

What is the 'Divine Principle'?

Simply, it is the cognitively available understanding we can reach of the originating heart of desire for relationship, of God, as suggested by a proper understanding of Jewish history; the indicated behavior translated into such form as to offer an unconditional support for all others, sustained under all conditions, & in all environments.

What should confound the theist is exactly what this 'God' offers humanity, IF we are listening... & IF WE care. History told us, but we didn't get it then, nor since.

Dare I suggest, as an atheist, that 'God' has provided humanity with the tools, purpose & means to realize our fullest potential, as individuals & as a species? IF God exists... but...

As I have established elsewhere, the issue of God is NOT an issue, UNLESS WE make it an issue. Really, folks, the issues of life emerge from our own mirrors. When we truly engage that person staring back at us… with suspicion, we might note.

But if God does provide the tools needed? Then I MUST offer THAT evidence. Because, God or not, it is what history has bequeathed me & thus, I myself have inherited, for the value indicated, as potential & as history offers is possible.

Quite conveniently for all of humanity, Jewish history still speaks for, & to all humanity, & still offers all the same moral insights & conclusions & needed direction for a restructuring of our own core values, as both individual wisdom, but also as wisdom to serve the whole species. Conveniently, our families are also the prime beneficiaries.

Jewish history is actually a central figure in the universal human development of civil morality, intended for a whole people, but universally applicable & rational & rationally accessible by all humanity. Both for its universal value but also universal applicability.

After the integration/intervention of God realized through Moses, the Jewish people were united not just by a promise, but now, they were to be substantially & morally committed to one another, just as one would do in any healthy family. A human standard for both family & therefore civil society was co-created between the people & God. Even social evolution, & therefore historical restoration, was established as a socially significant norm.

The "GREAT" social obligation, meant to inform hearts, not just external behaviors, was that we were "to care… by loving God with all our heart, mind & soul, & by extension, our neighbor as ourself."

THIS IS THE MEANING OF FAMILY. MY FIRST NEIGHBOR, OBVIOUSLY MY PARTNER... THEN OUR CHILDREN. NO LESS NEIGHBOR, FOR THE VALUE DEMANDED & EXPECTED. NOT AS A MATTER OF LAW, BUT OF HEART, AS IS INDICATED. ALL OF OUR BEING... OFFERED. Surrendering to love for the meaning it creates, the reality it establishes, the experiences it generates as living memory.

All as an act of freedom, to be fully & truly human.

This is the 'science' of living, that is also the living witness & wisdom of the cosmos. Integration the key. Heart, (the will to be in sustainable relationship), the motivating source. Rationality the tool. Community... the fruit.

When this quality of desire is established as an individual norm, then ALL relationships are of intrinsic & absolute value. But there also are degrees of meaning, in the value of the impact they have upon our lives. Parenting & marriage are two most significant such arrangements of community life.

Yet, even in all the joys of integration with others, the emphasis is most often upon a mutuality of benefit, recognizable to both parties. A constitution exists between such parties, a constitution of commitment, integration & attendance. There is then a greater sense of a shared creation, of a mutuality of environmental creation that is morally significant in its resultant ecology. An ecology of integration & creation.

In raising children, though, a different sense of the self is inspired & finds itself seeking definition. We come to assume a quality of stewardship not only for the relationship, as we naturally do in equal relationships, but also assume a greater responsibility for the quality of experiences shared & the direction we ultimately seek to establish as a 'societal norm', for our family. In this, we come to also assume the role of 'provider,' in all the ways imagined & subsequently suggested by experience.

In this role, we associate an emotional significance to the very fact of the demands made upon the totality of our being; physical, psychological & political. This is in the form of a satisfaction… & joy, adding a quality of personal meaning to life, one's life & the life we are in attendance to, such that we feel a quality of creative completeness not realizable any other way.

Shared, the experience becomes a totality of potential meaning, that offers a lifetime of shared meaning & feeds our motives, to enrich & sustain such effort, in every way imaginable. Family life becomes a sacred experience, offering a means to social integration into a greater community identity available no other way.

Beloved family becomes beloved community.

Parent & child realize the purpose of life. Together.

The image & experience God had 'in mind' all along.

Chapter 10- The buck stops here...: Parentism & 'The True Family Values' as the 'science' of OUR civility, beloved community & the kingdom of heaven

"Science (from Latin scientia 'knowledge') is a systematic enterprise that builds and organizes knowledge in the form of testable explanations and predictions about the world." Wikipedia

"Science is the pursuit and application of knowledge and understanding, of the natural and social world, following a systematic methodology based on evidence. Scientific methodology includes the following: Objective observation: Measurement and data (possibly although not necessarily using mathematics as a tool) Experiment and/or observation as benchmarks for testing hypotheses." The Science Council

"God's truth is sent to earth as a revelation given through certain providential figures. God's truth is the absolute truth, which is an almighty key capable of solving any problem, no matter how difficult it may be... When this truth is applied to society, social problems can be settled, & when this truth is applied to the world, world problems can be realistically solved... This is a new view of life, a new view of the world, a new view of the universe, & a new view of the providence of history that has never before existed. It is also a principle of integration that can encompass the whole into one unity, while at the same time preserving the individual characteristics of all religious doctrines & philosophies." Rev. Sun Myung Moon

"Children need to experience The True Family Values, both as the normative experience needed to socialize any potential 'citizen' into their role as a contributing member in good standing, but also for the equality of social development it creates. This contributes to a normative cultural experience in which all the children experience the same standard of psychological building blocks needed for healthy, sustainable interaction & intercourse with others, as a peer." The Last Spiritual Samurai

If one has read this far, then there is no doubt, theist or not, religious personage or not, life requires, given human history, that we take more than a cursory look at our own lives, with an eye to a makeover of cosmic proportions. To have ANY measure of self-respect & pride, we cannot ignore either the unmet challenges of history that we contribute to, that we maintain in our mutuality of social engagement, in our own 'sinning,' nor can we afford to ignore the potential for human suffering to become worse than it is, if there is neither a confrontation with our challenges & a corresponding commitment to such principles of relationship, that a new form of social & political creation is the result of willed human integration.

The challenge is rationally recognizable, rationally accessible for those so inclined & suited up to the challenge. History, for once, is our friend. For history can now guide us with the wisdom gleaned from experiences not our own, but inheritable as our own. Those of us with more than a mere social conscience, who truly view all of humanity worthy of 'saving', are thus not only encouraged, we are also empowered to act as providentially significant historical actors, seeking to make a difference & prove, once & for all... all life matters. And, if needed to be said in this climate of denial & hate, black & others of color... & women no less than ANY other; if one matters, all matter.

It is no accident to call The True Family Values as science.

Parenting, as an accident of midnight encounters, or planned down to every detail, as much as is possible, parenting is also a moral encounter of both need & potential that is always beyond the expectations of the actors involved, but provides the supporting environment where we discover new potentials we didn't realize we had.

With any child, there are always degrees of inherent vulnerability that come with living... & maturing. Maturing represented by the quality of sustainable integration we can manage, with or without support. Babies have a quality of dependence not experienced except under such extreme conditions of vulnerability. This is a significant challenge to our commitment to always be prepared, always ready. As every 1st time parent discovers, especially, in this sexist world, women often discover, alone.

As children become more mobile, then their perchance to not only make new discoveries is enhanced, it is multiplied beyond the imagination of simple parents to always anticipate & prepare for, if preparation is even possible.

Hence, the 1st principle of parenting is in the quality of the commitment we make to the whole enterprise…child, child rearing, child resource acquisition, procurement & subsequent management become 24/7 tasks.

This has moral significance. For the child, in the totality of the environment we create, psychological/spiritual & physical, & the means we use to continue the process of maturing in our children. The means being the values we employ, as a living example & as a living experience & hence, the world such values describe & demand of us, as participatory social agents, of more than a casual moral significance, to the outcomes sought or realized.

That generation after generation, of every religious, geographical, ideological or genetic predisposition, all have relied on the same essential value orientation, as parents, parenting, to produce a universally recognizable foundation for both civility & integration, argues that we have discovered a 'science' of child rearing, that has common elements that define the means & fruits to be realized.

1st & foremost is the indication of the need for a quality of sustainable commitment is needed as is not needed by most any other social grouping, except those in bad health or affected by age. Hence, a commitment to a quality of sustained attendance & integration requires a reasoned, however realized, consciously or just as some unconscious emotionally significant evolution, a reasoned commitment to care.

This use of freedom, to rationally plot a moral course & then seek to sustain it as the measure of the who, what & how we are with others, is also a measure of the maturity of the commitment to care we are engaging to meet this new opportunity. This becomes a pattern of disciplined engagement, that represents the 'best practices' for the results desired & sought, both for the child & the parents.

As parents, we realize that what we hope to impart, to teach, must also match our own motives & behaviors. Hence, the 'science' of living itself is offered. The effects upon environment, both in people & our effect upon the physical environment, then becomes the ONLY form of persuasion to impart our values to our children, that is both morally valuable but also the living witness to its value, to the individual & to the group as a whole system.

In the process of incorporating a cognitively recognizable moral means of integration, children pass through various stages of both cognitive potential & emotionally significant integration of the role & value of relationships. In the beginning, children mostly learn by obedience as the emotionally compelling social response to our parent's direction. But even obedience is not enough to prevent either errors of judgment or harms from a pure lack of experience.

This then requires a form of corrective behavior from the parents. This correction can take place both rhetorically or by example, or, most often, by the inclusion of both strategies, to more clearly educate to the norms needed. This then requires a new attitude on the part of the parent. This is the initial significance of forgiveness.

Forgiveness is a strategy of coherent, rational behavior we offer to the experience of deviance & the individual responsible. It is the acknowledgement of the deviation, but in such form then as to seek both the means to immediately address the situation, as well as offering the sustained commitment to act as an aid to the restoration of both the individual & the relationship affected.

Forgiveness then is the original commitment then contextually reinterpreted to meet the needs of the ongoing potential for relationships. Forgiveness then acting as behavioral evidence of a strategic move to save a relationship threatened & damaged. Forgiveness embraces such a vision of self, & others, as an extension of self, that the act imparts a protecting sense of the value of others, even in conflict; that is there is no other recourse than to carry forward with the quality of care initially offered, now merely reformulated to be contextual towards restoration.

Forgiveness then is a word to describe a state of reasoned & rational commitment, that can carry us past the emotional significance of events, to always defend people & relationships, even with our enemy.

Forgiveness is the 'science' of applied morality, morality merely the social recognition of the personal, public & political significance of relationships. That we take into account of, in our social wanderings.

Repentance is the response we have to the cognitive recognition & acceptance of not only a morally significant deviation in the social norms, but it also not only owns such responsibility as is indicated, repentance is the embracing of a quality of shame that motivates one to corrective effort. Repentance then the 'science' of making such offering, both in values & in subsequent behaviors, as to establish a new environmental ecology, one that now supports not only community, but beloved community.

Every person, every family, every religious association, every culture, every nation, every race, every sexual orientation… all employ these fundamental values, even if expressed both in form & quality in a broad spectrum of potentials.

The ONLY variance is in the forms they may take, as cultural, national forms or in the quality of moral intent inherently offered as part of the experience.

Jesus observed that there was no greater love than one lay down their life for another.

Jesus understood that.

It is what he taught was the defining value that expressed all that God had offered as experience & expectation… of humanity, as God's children.

Jesus taught that God had never betrayed humanity, rather walking every step, with each person, & with all. Jesus called God 'father,', a suggestion of a quality of experience & commitment that humanity could understand, could relate to. Hence, Jesus also implored the people to allow a quality of intimacy & vulnerability to be realized, to allow God a greater impact in our lives, by seeking to live as God lived… loving all others.

This was the standard Jesus offered was the natural experience of 'being Jewish' & thus, required a correlative qualitative response from humanity. Not in some small part for the offering God was seeking to bequeath to humanity, as need & potential both dictated were critical to human well-being. God sought to offer humanity the insights

154

critically needed, to evolve beyond the social reality they were creating with one another, for the lack of a better strategy & the heart to realize it.

We observe, in the evolution of moral history that was the Jewish experience, a developing moral structure of such a particular form that today that pattern is easily recognizable. But we have a luxury not shared by those at those times. They only had a quality of intuition & rationality matched to their normal needs & experiences.

God, or Jewish moral/civil evolution, creating such tensions about the significance of relationships, to be successful in morally reorienting humanity, in part or whole, the pattern & it's internal meaning & social value MUST be rationally recognizable by all humanity.

Hence, it must also be systematic in its natural considerations. Systematic in its application.

Love, as parenting or merely as the daily revelation of our way of being with one another, becomes a rational statement of intent carried forth into behavior.

The values are important to one purpose… establishing morally significant, sustainable relationships. The nature of their application allows both a quality of individual expression & freedom not realizable any other way. Hence, if the science is 'done right,' the results are both predictable & controllable.

The 'problem' in human history is the quality of needed commitment is not controllable from the outside, like some piece of programmable equipment. The result is both the uneven application of such values & equally, the confusion as to what standard should exist.

What should it mean to 'be human'?

Our ONLY 'scientists' have generally been on the one hand, vague about what is needed, but on the other

155

hand, uniform in the qualities needed. But universally, they expressed less than 100% confidence in either our heart for the task, or our willingness to understand & seek truth & its wisdom... the truth of how to live.

ONLY 2 such 'scientists' suggested they knew the scientific 'formula' needed by humanity, to reverse the course of human history. But they BOTH argued that we, humanity, will find no peace until we make the commitment to be TRUE SCIENTISTS of the HEART ourselves.

The result?

Parentism... the science of civility... the promised kingdom.

The True Family Values... their potential & real value considered

The True Family Values establish a universal standard of relationship, both as a natural human enterprise, & as a standard for parents, to socialize the next generation into a social arena where our value is determined by our integration into morally significant sustainable relationships, rather than just our secular, insular individuality.

The True Family Values spark a degree of creativity, of individuality of social expression, wherein 'beloved community' are it natural fruits. Hence, a psychological healthy & stable society for its degree of natural integration.

The True Family Values are timeless, universal & non-religious.

The True Family Values have been advanced in some form throughout all human history, therefore, they represent the core of human concern, need & sense of proper values for creating community. They represent, in our maturity of expression, our 'psychological/spiritual health'.

The True Family Values are sexually neutral. They emerge from the core of identity, the capacity & desire to care, & to be equally responded to.

The True Family Values offer the core values needed for ANY quality of relationship, to self, others, or the political & natural environments.

The True Family Values are the ultimate economic system, profit not the motive, but the offering we place before all relationships. It is the economics of sustainable co-creation.

The True Family Values are good 'science', based upon experience, experimentation & analysis of fruits desired & the ONLY means to realize them.

The True Family Values are the natural path to the social civility needed to both honor 'all are created equal,' but also to reveal the living witness of the citizen/patriot...

The True Family Values are the final confrontation with all other ideological rationalizations. No capitalism, no communism, no racism, no sexism or other rationale for slavery & human manipulation, offers equal freedom for all, freeing humanity from the spiral of history that never ends... only coils upon itself, generation after generation.

The True Family Values recognizes & affirms the natural kinship of all humanity, as one global family. The True Family Values, offered to & by us as a species, or as children of God, the social fruits are of the same quality.

The True Family Values are the clarified pathway to The Tree of Life.

The True Family Values fulfill the promise of the Torah.

The True Family Values unite heaven & earth... to create heaven on earth.

The True Family Values creates, & sustainably establishes, as a national norm, '**Parentism**,' the heart of a parent, carried into the totality of life & living.

Parentism is the future of humanity... but it starts... as it should, in the family, in the heart of each parent. It starts with me. Creating the substantial image & experience of God, the 1st parent. Offering THAT... even to my enemy.

Chapter 11 - "I feel, therefore I am, hence, all that matters": Mastering my unprincipled emotional 'God' impulse

"The reactive mind (emotions) is a portion of a person's mind which works on a totally stimulus-response basis, which is not under his volitional control, & which exerts force & the power of command over his awareness, purposes, thoughts, body, & actions. Stored in the reactive mind are engrams, & here I found the single source of aberrations & psychosomatic ills." L Ron Hubbard

"...when there is intense verbal abuse against groups because of race, religion, nationality, or language, it becomes difficult, if not impossible, to maintain the principle & practice of freedom of speech." Robert A Godwin

"Before anything can be reasoned upon to a conclusion, certain facts, or data, must be established, admitted or denied." Thomas Paine

"For the white to lord it over the black, the Arab over the non-Arab, the rich over the poor, the strong over the weak or men over women, is out of place & wrong." Islam, Hadith of Ibri Majah

"no man is worth his salt who is not ready at all times to risk his body... to risk his well-being... to risk his life... in a great cause." Theodore Roosevelt

"Rabbi Yohanan ben Zakkai said, "Just as the sin-offering atones for Israel, so righteousness atones for the peoples of the world."

I must make a confession. This chapter, true to its subject matter, is not a chapter I take ANY pleasure in writing, may heaven forgive my arrogance. L Ron Hubbard, the creator of scientology & the prolific writer of science & speculative fiction, rightly identified the personal, public & social significance of unbridled, unowned & immorally principled emotional identities, loosed upon interpersonal relationships. His solution produced Scientology... a remarkable means to such emotional control & identity stabilization as to offer a quality of personal freedom seldom realized by people.

Unfortunately, it also unlocked Pandora's Box for many of its users. They became successful... but at all things where emotions might have betrayed one before. Now, the anarchist can justify a degree of interpersonal subjectivity as to come to control morally what is not justified, in contrast to a community where the political reality of all are created equal has placed every person so as not to be a natural profit potential to all others.

Emotions are by their very nature & purpose, in serving the body, one of indulgence & self-centeredness. The emotions are the result of an engagement of a physical part of the body. Emotions are not independent of the body, they serve as an early alert system & source of sustained energy, to respond to stimuli with, that which is environmental as well as that which is the result of our reasoning & reflection.

In the process of birth & identity formation, babies have no greater rational capacity than that expressible through emotions. There is no other vocabulary & the voice has not been trained in any formation of articulation other than that which just naturally emerges as baby sounds. Hence, the 'me' is most passionately experienced as an emotional rush in response to some stimuli. It could be internal, such as hunger, or external in needing 'mommy' to comfort one in a moment of insecurity.

The 'me' of living then is most significantly associated with 'I am feeling thus & thus.' This quality of experience is also directly affected by the effect of the nature of the priming values experienced as a child being socialized to the necessity & value of relationships.

If the emotional identity has been socialized by The True Family Values, then the child has experienced the quality of emotional identity career guided by such values. The sense of a 'natural right to authority' is offered as a moral normative experience in the parenting behaviors. Parents not only provide externally needed resources, but other behaviors that are normative for developing a psychologically healthy individual.

That can be as simple as smiling, talking to the baby.

As the child matures, physically as well as emotionally & rationally, the appeal to parental authority is to a portion of rationality, that aspect that argues for community. In such rational demarcations, children learn the purposes & limits of social integration & deviance. Initially, because the emotions are allowed the freedom most associated with the anarchist, naturally mind you, the challenge of parenting is to solicit a degree of willingness to correction, hence discipline, the social confrontation that what one has accomplished has somehow not met the mark & requires an adjustment.

As the child responds favorably to efforts as integrative social & moral redirection, several factors emerge. The commitment to a degree of rationality & it's needed standard of shared social engagement is established as a norm for the family, hence all individuals. This also establishes recognizable boundaries defining the beginning of deviance, IE, willful acts of emotional significance to all for its implied forced environmental impact.

As children exercise obedience, as compliance & habit, will, a rational use of human effort towards some value, becomes more focused & realized not only for its value, but also for its necessity to process the experiences now coming at hurricane rate. EVERY experience has emotional significance precisely because it is happening to me. Whether that produces good or bad emotions seem out of control for much of youth.

That is the challenge left in the failure to have the processing habits of True Family Values.

Yet, forced both by habit forming behaviors of obedience & compliance, emotional responses become more measured, both for their frequency as well as for the nature of the moral values informing & the form the behavior takes as social actions. Children also learn that emotional outbursts, while often seemingly comforting in the moment, are also a public display to bring either recrimination or support. Depending upon circumstance & the morals of those involved or affected, directly or collaterally. Hence, risky business at best.

In general, the movement is away from displays of emotions that indicate ONLY self-interest UNLESS the contextual morality of the situation would rationally argue otherwise.

But children unconsciously come to the realization... emotions are merely a vehicle for the range of emotional expressions we 'decide' is appropriate, unconsciously or not.

Emotions ARE measured... at least for the 'intended' meaning, if not the executed one. The rational use of the brain is where the REAL 'me' exists. For it is in such decisions where integration is indicated, that I act with such values as define the 'who, what & how' I am to be... with all others. 'I' chose what emotions are fitting.

But those 'fitting' emotions emerge as the fruit of the desires we entertain for integration & community. A decision-making process from beginning to end, no matter the quantity & quality of emotions entertained in the process.

I choose to love... or I choose to hate.

But not always in ways immediately recognizable.

Maybe not even recognizable to whom would deny.

Today, in America, lies are now brandished as somehow equal to truth... & to be accorded the same difference & honor. Truth & lie now to be not only indistinguishable but now to be equal… as if the same in meaning & social value.

This is as emotionally significant a moral development initiating a national crisis as America has ever faced, even with racism & slavery.

No one called slavery a living truth. But they tried to sell the lie.

They tried to call it moral, as if God's will, in lieu of such proper rationality as should be natural to human engagement.

Rationality is the means to ALL deviance, even if fed emotionally. The 1st act is always rational for the truly human whom chooses to love. If there is a physical problem with the body, a debilitating defect, this creates a differing moral paradigm. But deviance in humans is both rational & accidental.

The evidence of our rational use of freedom so far is the bane of human history. The emotionally significant decisions we have made, in how & why we will process relationships, argues in the reality we have created that we are psychologically pathological & a genuine threat to ourselves & ANYONE & ANYTHING we come in contact with, for a moment or a lifetime. Obviously, the accidental harms is dealt with differently as a moral social dilemma.

But the challenge is that we allow our emotional identity not only a full range of emotional indulgence, we also come to allow a corresponding degree of physical expression of both the emotional content, but also its interpretation as a physical act itself with its consequent impact on the environment.

What we felt becomes what we do, which is what we do to…

The challenge is the integrity of our commitment to care for others, interpreted as having such moral authority & sacred significance as to whom we want to be, that we offer our moral sensibilities through our offerings to be such that beloved community is its natural fruit.

This is the natural outcome to those who live The True Family Values.

Jesus lived to offer such values.

Yet, the people were not so committed.

They even violated the 1st commandment, the 1st covenant.

To love God with all their heart, mind & soul.

They didn't 'feel' like it.

We don't 'feel' like it.

Of course.

We don't 'feel' The True Family Values.

If truly felt… then our emotional identity is held to the standard of heart our social conscience argues is what we know love to be… no excuses.

No… "ain't NOBODY perfect."

Says the loser.

Who lost because they chose to not care, as a human. Who, in not caring, allowed a part of the body, the emotional part of the brain, to become the new ruler… the 'brain' for the identity.

A child never grows up.

Hell is created on earth… we have rationally agreed it should be so. Our emotions dictating this clearly.

Who's to argue with emotions?

Chapter 12~ Living as a 'true parent/patriot': Parentism as global leadership & defining our environmental stewardship

"That is the short & long of it..." Shakespeare

"What missions should the new truth be able to fulfill? The new truth should be able to unify knowledge by reconciling the internal truth pursued by religion & the external truth pursued by science. Consequently, it will enable all people to overcome the two types of ignorance, internal & external, & fully comprehend the two types of knowledge... Next, the new truth should lead fallen people to block the ways of the evil mind & to pursue the goals of the original mind, enabling them to attain goodness." Rev. Sun Myung Moon

"There is a cosmic difference between heart... & emotion. One is the capacity to care, the other a physiological response to stimuli, natural or artificial, physical in origin or interpreted meanings derived from experience. They can be integrated to create a complete experience of the timeless with the moment." The Last Spiritual Samurai "There must be no limit to your goodness..." Jesus

"Only those who are absolutely sincere can fully develop their nature. If they fully develop their nature, they can fully develop the nature of others. If they can fully develop the nature of others, they can fully develop the nature of things. If they can fully develop the nature of things, they can then assist in the transforming & nourishing process of Heaven & Earth." Confucianism, Doctrine of the Mean 22

"Leadership should not be a question of charisma, how the image affects us as an emotionally compelling component, but rather leadership should be contextually considered as a matter of principles to define motive, to inform & guide behavior. This demanded standard of behavior a sustained state expressed across all social mediums, personal, public & political. Leadership is ultimately about the principles of civility, of parenting & of social cohesion. Of community, as a morally significant integration of sacred individuals." The Last Spiritual Samurai

"The family is our 1st society. Parents, the first unforced, natural social authority. The original 'law' givers, defining limits, freedoms & social obligations/opportunities. The shapers & definers of tradition, social norms, the labelers of deviance & foundational creators of sustainable community. Culture is 1st created & emerges here. 'National' interests are defined & defended against foreign (outside) interests. The nature of the values to be used in various kinds & qualities of relationship are given definition & meaning. Experience is justified by cognitive reinforcement." The Last Spiritual Samurai

I have made the case throughout this exercise in moral reflection to be centering on the centrality of relationships to life, living & the consequences naturally emerging from such intercourse. Concurrent with this effort is the corresponding articulation & defense of The True Family Values.

While one must admit that these universal, timeless values have been defined & defended by every major thinker, educated or not, which naturally includes parents, their very image is the image of the needed socialization of children into ANY family.

What Jesus & Moon did for us was to clarify the EXACT standards to be applied, the consequential standard to be understood as the underlying key. Jesus & Moon both established exactly what values must inform our journey. This defended standard both their understanding of God, as a social agent in history, & the subsequent & corresponding surrendering to live & defend the same values.

As the totality of their offering to life.

In this sustained behavior, they exhibited all the characteristics naturally associated not just with a sibling, seeking to aid their family, but more acting as if on behalf of the parent, to assume such responsibility as opportunity & effort can realize. Offering for the parent, what the parent cannot offer, but would offer were God able to. In this, Moon & Jesus offered to be 'acting as if' to create the experience 'as it is'. Jesus & Moon sought that each person, in their experience of The True Family Values, would come to such a personal experience of gratitude, that the natural offering is to 'pass it on'.

Jesus & Moon, like Buddha, Gandhi, King, Rosa Parks, Albert Camus, Thomas Paine, Confucius, the Prophet & so many others, passing it on was part of the value of the inheritance. So, share as has been shared with. Pioneering for the sake of a future possibly more challenged, more heart-broken. Anticipating

Jesus & Moon both, as did all the most significant thinkers, from mothers to the theologian, all gave consideration to both the challenge before them, but also sought for the missing pieces of the puzzle, if there were any to be missed.

Lo & behold, now we know Jesus & Moon came to the final bridge, crossed it, & then, offered that if no other crossed it, there would be not be the social impact & meaning life & living required for humanity to evolve past the hell it has so far natured & nurtured through history.

The ONLY RATIONAL decision left? Make one's whole life the mission to help as one has been helped… & helped by that which helped originally. Offering the ALL that no capitalist would, for the loss of some imagined potential for profit.

THAT IS NOT ONLY THE HEART OF A TRUE CHILD, SEEKING TO AID THEIR PARENT IN THEIR EFFORTS, BUT A CHILD WHO COMES TO SHARE THE SAME QUALITY OF HEART, IE, COMMITMENT TO CARING. THUS POSITIONING ANY SUCH PERSON BEFORE ALL OTHERS, OFFERING ALL, WITH NO OTHER RESTRICTION THAN THAT WE LOVE OURSELVES NO LESS, EVEN IF AS AN ENEMY, OFFERING NO LESS TO OURSELVES THAN ANY OTHER.

Jesus & Moon call & liberate us ALL to a quality of attendance of heart not revealed in history as a sustained individual & social effort.

Every mother worked to realize such values.

Every religious teacher & prophet sought the same solutions, articulated the same core.

To care is to be human.

To so care is to be a child of God... or the cosmos.

If I commit to so care, that I express The True Parent Values as my way & means towards all integration, then I become a 'true parent' to my child or children, offering them the experience of such values as elevates the significance of human life to be that of heaven, rather than the hell we offer as an inheritance to our children now.

As a true parent, I would now observe the world differently. EVERY parent initially experiences some moment of clarity about the assumed opportunity. As a true parent, my commitment initiates a degree of concentrated awareness not needed before. But context demands its own morality. Morality then justifying its needed supporting behaviors.

Parenting no less than any other.

Then, if I am a true parent, then all things are under the authority of that value system. For it defines the me, in the moment, in the eye of the universe.

Parentism is born.

Parentism then defines the patriot.

As a parent, as a leader, as a citizen, as a patriot... as a child of God. All culminating in one moral commonality. The values that realize a living example of beloved community, principles of integration guiding the hearts & minds of people towards the same rational conclusion.

Humanity matters... because life matters.

Hence, everything that contributes to life is sacred to that value. Creation, the natural resources surrounding us, this is the begging point of a true integration.

Applying The True Family Values to our efforts at integration with the physical environment itself requires a maturity not rationally engaged... as yet.

The evidence?

Our nuclear capacity for global annihilation many times over & we sustain the threat as a real potential for us...

Further evidence?

The destruction & pollution of many of our various environments, all needed to serve life, not just human life.

The evidence of the willingness to destroy is still at an immature level?

Leaders imagine war as legitimate for any human engagement. Willing to shed blood, not their own, in causes best left to schoolyard sandbox bullies than an international environment threatening all life.

Yet, it is still considered rational to war for any reason. Wealth of some kind is indicated such that other human life is not too high a price to pay.

Parents, true parents, could never blindly support a nation or world with such values. Such a parent would cry for EVERY starving baby, ANYWHERE.

True parents could not abide ANY OTHER PARENT HAVING TO SO SUFFER FOR THEIR CHILDREN.

True parents would imagine the creation, its natural & created resources, as a trust, not just for consumption, to fulfill some twisted idea of freedom. True parents would recognize that consumerism is a 'sin' against all that life is & all that life can be... for humanity, too. We should mimic the creation. If we want life to continue, then it needs the quality of attendance & such correlative 'nutrients' as to insure the greatest 'harvest.' But as a sustainable effort, for a sustainable needed future... as parents normally make efforts towards.

But now we need to do it as a global statement of attendance to what it must mean to be human, to provide for a human future.

Hence, rather than our remaining as local parents, as part of a global community, we need to acknowledge that integrated reality, even if we don't act mature & integrated. Parents who imagined a world nurtured & natured by The True Family Values could not imagine other families being any less deprived or hindered than themselves. Emerging in a nation already demanding a public conscience that honors all others as equal, such parents would immediately extend that value to all others.

Recognizing the need for a global attendance to The True Family Values as a needed recalculation of human potential & responsibility, such parents would naturally join with all others, Parentism the natural social & political expression of their behaviors, as citizens & as emerging global patriots.

For any true parent would never imagine any child should suffer any more than their own. No true parent would imagine squandering resources for consumption, just to produce profit, to marginalize & create an economic elite that cannot naturally therefore also support all as equal.

Further, no true parent would imagine utilizing resources for consumption beyond the pale of what is needed first to support human life… psychological no less than physical.

The True Family Values lived provide the ultimate supporting environment for any child, anywhere, under any cultural or religious narrative. Hence, my Japanese-America daughter could marry an African who had been raised with the same values & their children would naturally emerge mature anywhere they were raised.

Exhibiting a maturity recognizable anywhere.

Whom truly cares for others will eventually reveal themselves. The noonday sun is that unforgiving. But that noonday sun reveals all things…

Even evil seeks the light, to expose & argue itself as 'mattering.' For what evil was created in darkness, now demands equal time in the sun. As we observe in some current political behaviors that demand lies should be considered morally equal to truth & reality.

But the noonday sun also reveals what was hidden, what is even now denied. What is not loving, is not loving, never was, cannot be sold as such.

The Antichrist may try.

But in the birth of a global Parentism, the sense of the genuine desire & sought-after opportunity to care, behaviorally attached now to the use of the creation itself, reveals the true parent versus the false parent.

For the true parent, the creation is not some profit center yet to yield to 'me & me alone' some benefit, that I can then exploit over others. The earth becomes 'HOME".

HOME.

That sacred place, sacred above even a church.

Home is where FAMILY is.

ALL THE SURROUNDING 'PROPERTY' NEEDED FOR THAT DESIGNATION IS THUS ALSO HELD IN TRUST… FOR FAMILY.

Earth is home to ALL God's children… & the children of the cosmos. Lest anyone not recognize that if God exists, we are all family; if not, the sentiment is still rational & the underlying moral logic demanded perfect for human consumption. Be damned any authorship.

Parentism is then the political statement of my commitment to a standard of interpersonal values that will ONLY morally support community that recognizes the sacred value of all life, human life no less nor any more than any other, even considering the child of God potential status we are encouraged to embrace, behaviorally.

Parentism is my values taken to the world, as my offering to its conversation. Parentism is my music offered in the dance of protection & attendance now offered not just as normative… but now offered as natural. Parentism is the extended commitment to the totality of the social & political environment, what one had committed to in a limited environment.

Parentism recognizes 'family' as a group whose values & experiences create a baseline quality of experience that then defines the nature of not only the immediate relationships, but acts as the North Star for all future such engagements.

Parentism acts like the same quality of glue that a Jew experiences in knowing that wherever one might go, & encounter other Jews, one knew a quality of family existed even there that could not be diminished by the absence of being truly 'home'.

'Home' then for a true parent will be anywhere others are that then are as true parents. We will discover, as Jew or global citizen, the Gentile family, the atheist equivalent, our Muslim family, our Hindu family, all living the same values, as well all the others that color the human experience. Everywhere we will go, family will emerge... like blossoms responding to the light of day & opening to gather its resources & offer its beauty.

When nationals engage True Family Values, their Parentism will make them passionate defenders of not just their neighbors, but even viewing those seeking refuge in America, or any where else where home no longer exists, such people will be viewed with the compassion that speaks to their needs... not our sense of now having to share our resources.

People who immigrate, with no other resources than what is on their backs, HAVE NO FAMILY.

America promises to care.

ONLY FAMILIES TRULY CARE.

America's people will be judged, not accused, by the promise of 4 little words.

True Parents, in their native Parentism, will of necessity arise to the occasion. No joy, no sense of loss... except for the sense of what the people before us, OUR FAMILY, have lost.

In most cases, everything.

True parents cannot suffer ANY child suffering, true parents cannot abide ANY mother bereft the resources she needs to care for her children.

ANY man who would argue otherwise, & not so provide, as a leader, of this nation or any nation, should be run out of office.

Yet, today, in America, the Republican Party is revealed as against Parentism.

Yet, the party is made up of parents, with children. The solution?

We need true parents to be leaders, who will advance Parentism. Parentism… the future of patriotism.

Musings...

Christ VS Anti-Christ: The simple equation

"Love your enemy, that ye reveal the children of God..."
Jesus

"Be ye therefore perfect, as your father in heaven."
Jesus

It might seem questionable to include what appears to be a purely religious idea & juxtaposition it within these pages as an idea that even the secular & non-religious communities will need to consider.

It's actually based upon a quite simple logic.

What is good for religious people, seeking to live in morally significant sustainable communities, is actually equally good for non-religious, & even us atheists.

There is no form of life that is completely independent & self-sufficient. We all exist & thrive in various forms of ecologically formed environments. Relationships, sustainable relationships, yet flexible in the nature of their development, relationships are the key to all life.

It seems all the observable 'material' of the cosmos is somehow already primed to the potential for relationships, even if their forms & particulars are to be worked out environmentally, as potentials are exposed to such environmental support, that it can not only emerge, but become a stable feature of its existence.

The final witness of the cosmos, as evidence to the personal & species significance of relationships, is revealed in the human eye. Alter the relationship of a few molecules & maybe the eye isn't quite what it is. Maybe we do not observe colors. Or everything is lightly fuzzy, not clear-edged as we seem to observe it. The point being, whatever the evidence of life, it witnesses to the success & inherent value of relationships to not only the emergence of life, but its sustainability as an environmental factor.

Relationships, of a particular moral quality, are the ONLY purpose life seems to support. The continuation of such opportunity as individual potential & environmental resources can supply & support.

For humanity, the evidence is in.

WE ARE NOT FREE OF THE SAME IMPERATIVES THAT DRIVE LIFE SUCCESSFULLY.

Human life is sustained & enhanced, as a physical & psychological reality, by the quality of interpersonal values informing our motives & subsequent social behaviors. Our physical, environmental needs are not actually greater than the needs we have for meaning & personal fulfillment. They are more immediate in their priorities for life & living, but even in the most suffering of moments, it is the meaning assigned to such experiences that drive human history to seek solutions to the very problems encountered in the human use of freedom. Today, relationships are the key to our self-imposed hell & they are potentially also the means out of this created hell we have proudly used our freedom for.

When considered contextually, The True Family Values then emerges as the solution waiting for those not faint of heart.

For to love enemy, to repent & offer substantial & relevant change in one's values & social integration, is no mere decision for what flavor ice cream to order. For here, we are ordering our lives in a new way.

We have given the 'title' for such individuals who offer to humanity the solution to its most pressing problems... 'messiah'. The 'Christ'.

Yet, simply understood, what the messiah, what the Christ offers us, is a renewed understanding of human potential, as revealed when such values are applied to all potential relationships, even those in which deviance & harm have occurred.

Jesus calls us to a repentance of renewed values & their corresponding social expressions. Jesus offers us that faith is what we now offer each other, as our offering to God.

The original 'divine principle' now our own grounding value, then repentance & forgiveness are merely challenges to the discipline of 'heart' needed to own such values, as the source of our 'God-sense' offered to others.

In the restoration of The True Family Values, as an offering of 'Christ', as an individual acting to save his siblings from the habits of ages that produce hell, the 'Christ' merely acting as an elder sibling, then offering the wisdom of ages. All this to create such an ecological system of relationships, that beloved community emerges as the totality of the environmental fruits of human effort & personal discipline.

Hence, we are called to 'love our enemy', no less than God has loved us, as a measure of both gratitude & a child emulating the best of their parent, because it's the best there is.

But just as there are those inclined to seek all life offers, in moral opportunity & in the nature of possibility of relationships, there are those who are equally predisposed to 'not care'.

Capitalism, as an economic means to measure the value of relationships, does so ALWAYS & ONLY in terms of recognizing potential profit centers & then morally justifying any opportunities to act on that potential. Hence, even families are run on such a system of value, though variably so because of family, religious, cultural & political difference, yet in all, profit is still the underlying & most often, unowned hidden bias & value.

Hence, children can be property to parents, rather than a blessed opportunity to experience all of life's greater moments. A wife can be property, to be ordered & treated as a commodity to serve a purpose; sometimes personal & pleasurable, but not established for its potential to serve as a center for developing human happiness & meaning.

The 'Christ' then appears to offer clarity on the values needed by every person, every family, every nation, that the quality of interpersonal values & relationships we imagine should reign, will reign in the hearts & minds of a restored human value paradigm.

SO WHAT IS THE ANTICHRIST?

The antichrist is the individual, & in this case, also the whole family, who seeks both in living & in every rhetorical engagement, the profit center is to benefit they & ONLY those like them, every other person a potential profit center.

The means to such profit as to fit the situation, legality, morality, social custom, the cultural norms of sacred & profane all come under a concentrated & absolutely sustained behavior, a living statement of one value & one alone... the self.

For such individuals, moral is what profit is realized in any relationship, no matter how accrued, as long as it is kept. With no significant social consequence... except support among such a cult as would honor such publicity.

In keeping with such self-defining priorities, there is no commitment to such originating & guiding of national principles & values as is articulated in demanding we recognize & respond to one another as if an equal creation, hence, deserving of a corresponding civility so as to not only reveal that equality as an expression of personal behavior, but that it will also be recognized & defended in the public & political arenas. This because to be equal must also have its civil & political equivalences.

The antichrist flaunts & declares a 'right' to such antisocial values as to deny others that equality. This 'right' is an assumed entitlement as such, not as a result of some Constitutional wording or reading, because it is not there.

It has been shared elsewhere the psychological assessment that there is a 'dark-side' to human freedom & personality development & it's social expression. These characteristics are all anti-social in nature. They exist as an idea of a 'right' to exclusionary values & their behavior. They are based upon an assumed entitlement & arrogance as to one's deserved social status, as opposed to the general populace, of any community.

These values demand we imagine EVERY person & every social opportunity an opportunity for personal profit to be realized. Getting the better piece of something, the bigger piece, getting what others can't have; all sense of a self not obligated to community, for the failure to offer any such commitment.

In such personal posture, there is no love for others. There will be no repentance… for any harms created, by will & design or by happenstance. There is no forgiveness, no love attempted to aid the enemy to be restored to healthy community. There is no repentance that heals both parties, deviant & victim.

The antichrist will seek to be a leader, both justifying the deviant, anti-social values as a feat accomplished in the trail of tears left behind them in the people affected but not restored to a common community health.

Trump is the living & providential example of the current, PERFECT ANTICHRIST. He pretends to be a Christian. Yet, in a perfect witness, he offers, in behavior, all the values that are 100% in opposition to The True Family Values.

In his leadership, Americans, the religious right & their secular counterparts, are now regaled, from the White

House, on the values that ANY person can use, since the president of the United States uses them.

Today, BECAUSE 2 PEOPLE CAN AGREE TO MAKE A LIE STAND AS TRUTH, AMERICANS IMAGINE THAT FREEDOM OF SPEECH IS THE AMERICAN VALUE SYSTEM THAT ALLOWS SUCH AN ILLOGICAL & IMMORAL TRANSFORMATION.

Today, in our world, a lie, accepted & advanced as the 'truth' by one individual, then advanced & accepted as the 'truth' by a 2nd party, now has become un-challengable.

Today, if people declare a lie to be true, they falsely imagine the Constitution not only protects such a right, it actually justifies it as an American protected right, equal to all other rights.

THAT IS THE LOGIC OF THE ANTICHRIST.

THAT ANY MORAL QUALITY OF FAMILY & INTERPERSONAL VALUES ARE EQUAL TO HUMAN USE & THE FREEDOM TO BE ENGAGED. The success being whom gets away with it, is justified for its use. Criminal, president, parent, husband or boss. The antichrist values work anywhere humanity is available.

The antichrist seeks to destroy each person, as a morally significant factor to all relationships, in the 'right' to be exploited & it be justified as moral, for the anti-social individual.

When this anti-social phenomena is exploited on a national level, & with those held to a covenant with Jesus, based upon his revelation of The True Family Values, then those whom support that person, applauding the use of anti-family values, those religious people have united with the 'antichrist'. When that person can convince people, that in reality, much less America, that a lie is now equal to the truth & should be defended as such, then those people are following & uniting with the self-revealed ANTICHRIST TRUMP.

The ANTICHRIST has terrible significance for those Christians & other morally inclined people. Acting in accord either with Trump in support of such politically &

spiritually & providentially significant actions is to elevate evil to a national & international value... to be emulated & repeated. As the moral right & freedom of any people, who choose to honor freedom in such form.

That then become the vision America offers the world, the vision of the value of the individual... one now defined by a naturally adversarial value orientation, just as sure to destroy the family, as any individual. Those who are victimized, like most of white America presently feels, will never recognize the enemy who offers they are cared about... while ONLY truly doing for themselves.

The values of the antichrist ARE NOT religious values... they are 'perfectly' human. Satanic or evil, we are the sustaining authors, the master of the universe. But, lest we forget or assume too much...

True Family Values ARE NOT RELIGIOUS, NOT POLITICAL IDEOLOGY. Hence, it is as available to the atheist & non-religious as to any other.

But the True Family Values PERFECTLY confront the evil of the ANTICHRIST... AS A MAN, AS A FATHER, AS A HUSBAND, AS A CITIZEN, AS A FAILED PATRIOT, AS A LEADER... & NOT THE LEAST... AS A LOST CHILD OF GOD.

Thus, The True Family Values are the values every person can recognize for the social potential they offer in both individual & social engagement. Those who would seek to destroy such values as not for humanity, are acting against the personal & general interests of humanity.

The antichrist seeks for such social recognition, no less than the Christ, both in a social & political acceptance of self... but ONLY in the context of the offered values, so as to be handed the reigns of power, so as to do as one sees fit. Be damned convention, law, be damned equality.

Be damned tradition. Or family values. Hence, be damned humanity, except as slave or servant. ONLY.

The self is supreme.

What one can impose, take, & dominate to one's favor, all these are the successes of the antichrist. These are paraded as the successes others should envy & honor. Even if we can't really be like them.

The antichrist will use his own cult members as sacrificial offerings to his agenda. Their sacrifices his inherent right to use, without any accommodation or acknowledgement.

Hence, Trump offering nothing to help those insurrectionists who failed to truly do his bidding on January 6th. No bail, just attacks on the establishment for holding such people accountable to the law.

Which the antichrist does not support, but won't help his cult members either. Hailing them from on high.

Hailing them.

Nothing more.

That is the ANTICHRIST.

How do we defeat him?

Live The True Family Values… each day… with each other. As was always the ONLY purpose to life… & living.

Evil cannot choose to love… or it would no longer be evil. To love is to surrender… evil fears so much not being loved, hell will be created & sustained… forever, if needs be.

The antichrist will find much company, if there is life after death. But the time destined to be in hell?

Just as much as we choose now… by what we do.

Live as the antichrist living witness… or… live as a human. Being human. By the 'how' we are, with all other humans.

Simple formula for the Christ…all matter.

Simpler formula defines the Antichrist… 'I' matter.

Reflection

God's 'constitutional' socialism: A future home for all peoples, as family

"If freedom is to be extended, it must discipline itself both personally & communally. On a personal level this means developing a unity of purpose so that choosing & action are harmonious for the self. This also involves a communal awareness & concern, for the individual is part of society. Thus, unity has normative features in conjunction with freedom." John K Roth

    If, as an atheist, I must submit to seek community with all others, religious & non-religious, then I am to seek for a quality of interpersonal values as to most effectively create such a shared state of willed civility that we cannot imagine to do harm to one another.

    The 1ˢᵗ 'society' is the family. Within the family is the foundation for all nation states. Management, or call it government, the accepted responsibility, understood or not, creates a covenant. "We act now, this way, that the future will be of value to all, while acting in the interim so as to provide for the needs of the individual. This offering no less such support that the whole in no way suffers a privation for the needs of any."

    The family, if led by truly mature individuals, will have committed to such values as to provide all the support needed for children, spiritually/psychologically, as well as socially & physically. The most universal true family values are merely those values that when integrated into the emotional matrix of our emotional identities, provides the most proactive means to respond to the moral challenges of human intercourse. A humanity living in such proximity & having such needs, needs that are best addressed as communities, then the least rational considerations would nominally offer that wisdom would dictate a genuine need for a focused reflection, a meditation, as individuals, families & even nation states & religions, on how we can participate so as to create morally significant, sustainable communities.

The most socially simple family, the most socially sophisticated family, the rich family, the poor family… all face the same inevitability. The need for community requires a focus beyond the mere interests & needs of the one. As parents act in such fashion, as their living statement, as to the who they are & how they are in their integrative efforts, the offering of self to a greater whole emerges & dominates the effort.

This is not in the way of our families globally, in all the possibility it poses for a value needed orientation beyond the family. For the true family values are of such a focus that it is natural to extend oneself to all parties, with the same quality of intent to be of benefit. The commitment of each parent then the measure of them as humans, being human.

Since the global & universal sense of self as a human requires us to explore relationships for all their potentials & possibilities, then as parents, all the days of raising socially uncommitted children to the value & need for healthy relationships becomes a living exercise.

Since immaturity breeds immature consequences, then the measure of this as a social consideration is created in the resultant impact that must naturally occur. Thus, parents are challenged in at least two ways, first to stop the damaging/offending behavior, both to confront it in the prime of its expression, but also to mitigate & manage any resultant harms, to person & environment.

The challenge then for parents is to aid in the cognitive understanding of the child, to help impress not only the import of the moment, but also educating for a more developed awareness of ourselves as morally significant social agents… significant in the non-neutrality of our existence to those around us, the environment we share & the social/psychological ecology that must be co-created, to create a 'society.'

In the mature socially adept human, then the skills to aid such children then require we keep so committed that even in the event of deviance, our commitment to ourselves in this capacity to care emerges as the revelation of our social skills to remain focused on the need of the other. This to process the events but also to support the offender in such form as to act as a guide back to the values that will re-create the quality of interpersonal community sought.

When our hearts are truly in such efforts, to act as an aid & natural benefactor, then there is a subdued joy in the opportunity.

The joyful affirmation the other matters that much. The joyful affirmation of the opportunity before us, to affirm the value of this person, by aiding them as if they are all that matters. Remember the old wisdom… do onto others as. Yet, it is merely a unique version of ourselves before us under such circumstances… a 2nd self. Loving them then is also as if we have loved ourselves. It is a moment of creation.

Even as the behaviors of deviance create harm & potential chaos, our sense of proportion will also lead us to act as an aid to the harms & those harmed. Hence, we will suffer for what is, even as we seek remedy. But it is a natural impulse. Once each 'crisis' is normalized & children restored in the moment, then our focus as parents is the continuation of our effort both to attend to the needs of the children, but also to act with such forethought as to prepare for the future, seeking to anticipate both environmental needs as well as providing for the needs of children to effectively integrate into all the varieties of community that life both offers & demands.

Yet, the challenges of parenting are no less the same quality of challenges we all face, as a social group, be it a nation, a church, a political party, a government.

What makes one family more ideal than another? The quality of experiences possible & actually experienced. This standard of interpersonal means to relationship is the result of our individual & personal freedom utilized to create a rationale for willful integration. How much 'heart' is offered, as a sustained norm?

It is the heart of attendance, the heart of offering, that seeks community, that identifies the principled socialist family. The mature parent? Simply, a leader for any moment... ""Leadership should not be a question of charisma, how the image affects us as an emotional component, but rather leadership should be contextually considered as a matter of principles to define motive, to inform & guide behavior. This demanded standard of behavior a sustained state expressed across all social mediums, personal, public & political. Leadership is ultimately about the principles of civility, of parenting & of social cohesion. Of community, as a morally significant integration of sacred individuals... "

Utilizing The True Family Values, can we really imagine a better foundational image for leadership, be they a parent, a business owner, a senator?'

The true socialist mindset is the parent who is acting for the sake of all.

When our values, when the constitution we hold to, when they serve the greater whole, as to all, embracing all, then we have the meaning of 'family'.

As a nation created to be a social statement of integrated community, as its prime identifier, America demands we honor one another by accepting & embracing the moral imperative that, in fact, whether by God or by nature, all ARE created equal. Based upon that reasoned & reasonable affirmation of such a morally significant 'fact,' & the fact of the natural & intrinsic value of relationship, to human potential & need, then maturity & wisdom BOTH defend a stance that embraces all others as at the very least, 'extended' family.

Self-respect, or self-love, both argue for a degree of integration & intimacy that we co-create, that what we need to create, we do so together.

The world is not getting smaller.

It is getting more crowded, less room for errors.

We have reached such a density, where proximity is so normal an experience, that any harms to one are now also multiplied, both as effect & as affect on the psyches of the surrounding community.

No man is an island is no longer just 'hip' rhetoric. It is now life.

As such, the resources of the earth, in its parts & in its totality, must be reimagined as belonging to all of humanity, the future no less than the present. It is time for not only leaders to remember their role is that of a truly loving parent, but to now act like it, rhetorically, politically & as a life statement.

We must come to 'care' so much about human life, that the loss of one life is too many. Hence, each nation, harboring more of God's precious children, must be understood to be such children, worthy no less than our own children or the children of our enemy. Today, we must think like global parents, assuming a 'constitution' that demands we honor our own lives by how we honor all others. Thinking always about the needs of the individuals, the communities of individuals no less precious to the witness of life than any other.

As we assume a global 'parentism' in the heart of our commitment to care, to realize 'beloved community' in every opportunity, we are challenged to become new wine in new wine containers.

But then we also become obvious.

A parent always stands out in a crowd of children.

No matter how big the 'children' are.

The fact that the majority of Americans want health care for all, argues both economic arguments but also reflects the natural heart of every true parent.

That the 'leadership' refuses to acknowledge this clearly argues the quality of 'care' brought to bear by such leadership. That they & their families have life-time medical & the majority are independently wealthy, is also lost on the average American.

That America is the ONLY wealthy nation NOT to offer national medical argues medical as a consideration is not a genuine human need to be defined as a right, but a 'privilege' earned & paid for, as a focus of profit for others.

How can an American leadership refuse such facts?

By calling it communism, because THEY don't need such help, why should we? Even though they do not truly generate the wealth they manage, they do not understand the difference between their experience & the norm of the world.

They never will.

They can't

They refuse to have the heart of a parent towards any others than the small circle THEY support.

In such a world, racism, sexism & environmental abuses can rule because there is no one to be held accountable. Government representatives assumes powers over others, rhetorically as well as every way physically, so as to establish such a hierarchy of social values, with them at the top, that a generalized form of slavery is justified & enacted on every level imaginable & accessible.

Leaders every day are reported as exercising a prerogative to accept & demand 'better' for themselves first... living the self-centered slogan now touted as some form of patriotism... "make America great" by making "America First."

That is not a nation that honors "ALL are created equal"...

That is not a leadership that provides a national & global image of a patriot.

But I, for one, refuse to bow to such social pressures.

The 'Republican' conservative element of America no longer considers others equal.

For 50 years I was a Republican. The surgery to change hurt.

The right wing of America even demands separatism when they do not get their way. They support a lie, their leadership holding the 'great lie' up to the whole world to see... this is leadership?

Our nation now has joined the communist world & the world of dictators like North Korean & Russia because we declare that lies will be equal to truth, & no one dares argue otherwise...

EVERY SINGLE DAY OF THE WEEK, THE RIGHT WING AMERICAN MEDIA SUPPORTS TRUMPS BIG LIE, THEIR FORM OF JOURNALISM NOW NOT REALITY BASED, BUT NARRATIVE & MOTIVE DRIVEN. NO LOYALTY TO AMERICAN PRINCIPLES... JUST ANARCHY TOUTED AS PROTECTED FREEDOMS.

But today, among a great many of our more cognitively enlightened young people, is a thirst for righteousness... in our political behavior. That then demands a heart of attendance to the needs of the one & the many, in such form that the ONLY status is the joy of success, as we meet the needs of our responsibilities, to be human, by being human.

Today, the mindset needed most is that of a 'true' parent, a person committed to principles of relationship that prioritize a corresponding moral effort to manage all the resources of humanity just as any good parent would.

A leadership that is partisan in the nature of all its rhetoric & behavior, is a leadership also ONLY seeking to serve itself. It will place itself at the top of the benefit pile. 'America' 1st... the 1st always starting with oneself, never the bottom.

I am astonished when a Republican gets elected, & the 1st & only sustained commentary is one we observe that always degrades, marginalizes & continues the 'election' rhetoric towards non-Republicans, which argues that their representation in Washington does not include those who didn't vote for them... How does that work, as a moral statement of representing 'all' the people?

THAT America is the old America. The Jim Crow, the slave America, the witch-hunters & deprogrammers America. Where white is right...

But it is killing America today.

Starting with the people who are destroying it. THEY are the 1st victims. They were never taught the true values of America. Or the values taught by Jesus... Or any leader worth their salt. Hence, their every minute of life & living is a contradiction.

Only 'love' creates life & only love, as a human act, sustains it.

Like in the healthiest marriage.

As we act as 'true' parents in our families.

Acting for the sake of all in the family, each according to needs. Acting as a constitutionally informed & driven socialist. The parent/patriot, acting always as a co-creator to the reality of 'beloved community', the natural statement of family.

The future era of True Family Values: 2nd tier 'parenting' guiding & informing the 'helping sciences'

"Oneself, indeed, is one's savior, for what other savior could there be? With oneself well controlled one obtains a savior difficult to find." Buddhism

When my research, intuition & reasoning began to settle, I was shocked beyond comprehension as to a number of 'facts' I had 'discovered'. Even more shattering to my sense of self, as a totally independent feature of life, was that from my very 1st publication until this moment, a central theme & concept & conceptualization of human need & relief repeated itself in all the work. Now, some may call it merely my unconscious mind delivering what my conscious mind had not yet caught up to. That's a reasonable suggestion.

Now, I admit, the idea was pretty filled out, even consciously more than I realized at the time. But the ultimate centrality & inherent value it offered as an interpretation in the significance of the 'evidence' of God's 'behavior,' takes us into a completely new cosmos, one not easily inhabited by an unconstitutionally & morally inept & committed species of life, one critically dependent upon reason & principle for life & living, but not willing to so commit.

Insanity, really.

You scoff?

Have you REALLY looked around recently?

Or have you even met the 'man in the mirror' on a clear day?

It is obvious even to a madman.

I lived with my madness my whole life.

But I didn't miss YOUR madness in the process.

Being mad doesn't mean one is blind, deaf & dumb.

Yet, like the cosmos, change is the ONLY inevitable. What change may occur?

Today, I don't have hope.

Today I have confidence.

In the settlement of my mind as to the true & ONLY message & mission of the 'messiah,' a human like any other human, but unlike any other human, I discovered my own potential right in front of me. It was the same potential I had harbored the 1st time I intuitively asked, "Why am I not lovable?". Not only am I lovable, but my love is a value that is ONLY realized & offered to & in relationships. THAT need is also the fulfillment of human potential, the realization of The Tree of Life, the Fulfillment of the Torah, the path to peace.

WHY was it so important?

The True Family Values spell out the values & suggest the means needed to fulfill… with lots of practice.

But to a fallen humanity?

These values offer us the means to restore the past, by repenting it in the creation of a new reality, wherein beloved community is its natural outcome. In the engagement of others with this restorative effort, this accepting of the shame of the past, in the nature of the effort made now, we create new habits, the opportunity for a sustained way of being to emerge that establishes the foundation to realize the Tree of Life in our own being.

This potential, this possibility is also the challenge of a lifetime. To confront, in our hearts & minds, the faulty values of the past, that we might liberate ourselves to new opportunities. A new chance at self-creation.

Hence, if the average person is entitled, by the existence of a new but 'mere' opportunity, to realize a quality of being human not truly imagined or given effort to in humanity's past, then that means even the over-burdened, the forgotten, the abused & discarded, even we now have tools that can help us to find a new path forward, if only for the public support... a 2nd tier support in the flavor of parents.

Those of us exhibiting the more obvious flaws human abuse has marked us as 'deviant, those crushed in our human psyche, now can, with help, process the past that led us to this dark place in the sun. Where we can now recognize our own potential & needs in a healthy way, we can start processing the present in more healthy ways, which will unconsciously have the effect of weighing upon the past, by juxtapositioning our past with the current sense of self as we process experiences in ways we could not before.

The 1st principle, the Divine Principle, is the commitment one makes of the totality of one's being to all the relationships one will encounter. It is this initial unconditional commitment that defines the nature & quality of the subsequent values needed & to be brought into play to make that potential of relationship the norm, the natural, the inevitable.

This initial commitment, when challenged within a relationship with values & behaviors not conducive to beloved community, 'evolves' in such form as to seek to offer such support that the original potential can be still

196

realized. Hence, the nature of true forgiveness is not retreat & withdrawal, but rather a cognitively & purposely engaged posture of support & offering of contextually significant resources.

For those of us harmed in life, at a time when we had no other resources, or opportunities for such as we needed, we now can confront the demons of the past… our own & those offered us by others in the experiences they forced us to suffer.

Now we can act in our own best interest.

But this is ONLY possible when there is a social climate & social environment where in such values are understood, embraced, advanced & sustained as more than a mere therapeutic exercise.

But imagine for just one minute, psychologists who themselves have mastered or are mastering such values, as a socially affirmed value important to every citizen, be they child, parent or leader. Can you imagine offering those of needing therapy the tools that would allow us to process the past, even if we cannot change it.

I forgive my mother, my seeking to be of any service, any support to her own healing. Offered personally or offered even in just my living life as she would have truly wanted me to… By not being burdened & harmed by the past.

As I offer a living forgiveness, for a woman dead many years, I imagine her had she had such resources. Then, I am even more healed. For I know she would have eventually welcomed The True Family Values as I have. THAT too heals us as the abused. For we know the hell they occupied… in the hell they created for us. Who could not want release for such people? Even our worst enemy?

197

Would not the enemy, so freed from their own hate, also seek to heal the past, as they could? Even by helping another, we embrace the possibility of restoring the past, by the acts of faith now.

All of this argues that for the psychologist, for the prison reform advocate, there are tools that the people we attend need... They cannot get control of their lives, they cannot be any better, as moral & social creatures, unless they can come to imagine caring about themselves... by how they attend others.

That includes when WE harm, harming others, as much as when we are harmed.

For the unloved do not know how to love... for we weren't imprinted.

Remember?

Hence, we do not know how or why it is healthy to repent.

We cannot yet understand the value & meaning of forgiveness, also a means to our own psychological health. We also learn the meaning & value of good parenting & leading in such self-realization.

The True Family Values ONLY value is in their being our living statement, as citizens, defining the true nature of our patriotism. For the criminal, for the walking wounded, The True Family Values are the ONLY means to reclaim our humanity, an opportunity to be understood more in the nature of a civil right every person needs access to.

If we are to defend ourselves as civilized, as caring, as concerned about the inherited wealth & well-being of our children, then we also need to be equally concerned for all children to have the same quality of life experience we seek for our own. Logically, the ONLY way that can have more than a mere chance is when the whole society, from government representatives to our local religious centers agree such values are in the interest of all peoples, of any country.

Then we will have the pride needed to insure that even our prisons & therapeutic institutions employ such values, both as an aid to such people to better process the past, to become better in the moment, better in the personal & social significance of their offering to & participation in community, but also as the quality of experience now offered such conflicted people.

But no more will the therapist & the prison act as above the rest, for now, all will be envisioned in the same way. The therapist shares in the therapy, not from above, but beside, as needed. Parent, sibling, co-citizen... all working together to create beloved community. Be it a therapeutic moment or how we prepare cons to re-enter society & family life, the focus is on how we can be with one another... differently.

A parent/therapist is there to act as support & moral guide.

To our own potential to be fully & truly human.

Then, my neighbor matters to me, no less than my child.

Even then, the prisoner to be released?

Have we aided his experience, that he can have the tools that might lead him in a different direction in the processing of life, with family, work... & self?

When we accept that if we ARE going to help others, it needs be contextual help... not to just sustain them in society, not killing themselves or others, then we will seek for the wisdom that frees us from the past, to act with the maturity in the moment that reveals our true capacity for caring, uniquely, each according to their own imagination... of relationship.

Rather, we need to remember, God or no God, that is still 'family' out there... & in the mirror.

But what releases beloved community are The True Family Values.

Always what you need.

Always on time.

Therapist, prison guard, family or victim, we still all need one another. More to the point, we need to choose to allow that need & allow that opportunity to blossom & reach its own perfection.

The True Family Values are the solution.

But like all the best medicine.

It has to be shared... & then taken willingly.

The question is... will we choose to care enough to make the commitment?

Parent, child, spouse, therapist, criminal, politician, religious leader... there is one boat we are all in.

But we need a rudder... & a direction.

For the whole boat... & all its occupants. Even you & me...

History has heard us...

Ain't that grand?

We have The True Family Values... to process life with... to heal ourselves, & offering healing to others.

Parenting skills & values are universal... even an aid to therapy & liberating others from their pasts, to be free in the now, that there is no need for a future lifetime of therapy.

The 'therapy' will be HOW we CHOOSE now to love... with ourselves & each other. Therapist or client.

It's still the same damn boat...

Considering the future of political movement in America... to stay providentially viable to the world community

"No more just 'me & my world'... now it is us... & our world. The world you & I offer our children. To share... forever."

Most important change needed, that will come? The individual & social recognition of the wealth offered in The True Family Values, both as a social restorative agent, but also for the miracle of genuine & meaningful family, & therefore, community life it unleashes.

Today, even as immature as we are, as citizens, much less as the patriots we like to imagine we are, we MUST consent to imagine what future we need, as Americans, as humans; what future will satisfy us as both individuals but also as consecrated communities, seeking to create an integrated world.

We must thence move to 1st consider what needs change & why & what will serve to advance the cause of the human species, acting in concert with both individual need in mind, but also within the context of a greater whole. That whole including the totality of real, potential & possible future environments.

That America is off its own natural course, as dictated by the 1st principle of citizenship, that we are ALL created equal, hence, requiring more than a passing glance at our neighbor, (that to secure our right to the freedoms articulated & defended, we need to act in such concert with others as to secure a mutuality of environmental freedom, to be, to act,) we have long since abandoned that moral course.

Yet, wisdom & common sense should dictate that no man is not only an island, but our islands are in such constant movement, both internally, as in developing our individual nature further, & as in our natural movement as social beings, but is not the universally shared opportunity, personally, publicly or politicly, that we are now a crippled nation, & we blame everyone else for it.

Such constant movement naturally creates environmental contact. Such contact, on a physical level, if not moderated by some natural or environmental factors, can produce such friction as to be injurious to one or both parties. For humanity, this is managed by the nature of the defining moralities of the social actors themselves, both in how they view themselves, themselves in this environmental confrontation & hence, how they potentially view others, in the context of all needed considerations, real or merely imagined as such.

For humanity, there is such both need & benefit created by sustainable relationships, with their contextually created communities, that the value of a supporting moral paradigm for identifying both the value of the individual, but also that individual in community, adding to the value of that community, is natural & should become obvious to all caring people.

This was the moral significance of 4 words to be included in the Constitutional creation. Without those 4 words, no end to slavery, no voting rights for slave or women, no defense of Native Americans at all. Mexicans native to the land of the Americas, all non-white immigrants & all undesirable religious persuasions would then either suffer worse experiences of 2nd class treatment, or would be driven from our shores.

Those 4 words formed & informed the national conscience. Whether we honor that obligation of citizenship as a blessed opportunity to participate in the restoration of history, is the freedom that defines the line between the mere occupant of America, & her patriots.

So what kinds of considerations should we begin to reflect on & imagine as corrective? Let's consider a few...

First & foremost, we need the 'heart' that seeks reconciliation & restoration. We must develop our social conscience, that reflects the reality of a shared universe. We will need the 'heart' that can stand before judgement, not defending oneself, but asking how one might better serve, how one might aid the restoration. How one might change, to become the restoration... but also...

+A natural movement towards owning the worst of American history, that we learn from that history, not to sustain its impact of racism... by honoring the 4 words of the patriot... "ALL are created equal & so shall I act."

+In owning history, a national effort to recognize its injustice by declaring a National Day of Repentance for the Institution of Slavery & the Immoral Racism That Fed It.

+Movement towards securing all citizens within the economic protections that such a system should naturally provide. This to include such national medical that America will join the other economically advantaged countries who offer such to their own citizens, as a matter of life's needs, recognized as a universal.

+Movement will be made to understand America as a 'family' nation, from the individual family to the national level family, jealously protected by all her citizens.

+Movement towards a policy of environmental stewardship, to also embrace the idea that natural resources are also the domain of the greater community. Consequently, the uses to which natural resources will be allocated will also be a moral concern of proper attendance & management.

+Environmental impact of human life & living will be integrated into the moral & legal responsibility of nation.

+Freedoms defended, such as to vote, to secure such a protected environment, so as to engage such freedoms as are articulated & defended, by law or custom, will be at the heart of every citizen's behavior. My freedoms to act cannot be greater than yours. My freedom to impact the environment is not a secured 'right.'

+Economic behaviors will evolve… movement away from excessive salaries & entitlements for 'management,' be they employers, politicians, religious leaders, parents or any other such social forms, will become a moral norm. The underlying assumption, never owned in the daylight, the idea that more physical labor is to be equated with slave labor & therefore demoted in its social value, will be eased out. This last vestige of the Jim Crow era will be slow in evolving, but it must, or America will never be free of its past.

+A new quality of civics education will be offered. The past will be used, not to denigrate & belittle, but to learn from, since it IS our past. Hence, to gain wisdom from the past, in how we inform ourselves now. Thus, to always insure we neither repeat the past, but we also become a living act of both restoration & celebration; a celebration of the restoration of history we offer, securing a 'future' only imagined in the past, by so many. We live, that their lives now have the meaning they always should have had, but now can have through us.

+Movement will made from party exclusive politics to those who seek common ground & community, based upon long range goals for not only Americans, but the world. This requires a natural evolution towards a national recognition of the individual, family & social value of The True Family Values.

+A repurposing of the tax code to reflect the balance needed between corporate profit & tax responsibility to communities, to become part of those communities, rather than standing armies of profiteers. Always taking out of the 'community' what was created there. A profit not earned by positions, but by front line workers.

The people 'in the cotton fields,' not in offices, pay the price for profit. Hence, the 'greater' heroes & 'movers' will be the people who do the least inspiring, most physically demanding kinds of work. The dishwasher no less than the construction crew.

+The future will become the totality of morally demanded & protected environmental paradigms. We will no longer imagine profit for gratification, but work to meet need first. All human need. Everywhere.

+Sexism, racism, religious hatred, ethnic hatred… all will come to be viewed with shame, but the shame that insures, "never again…"

+Rhetoric will experience an evolution wherein our words are our honor, paraded before others, as the sign of our commitment to community first, anarchy last. Words will be recognized as morally significant behavior, hence, to receive a corresponding moral attendance.

+Resources, be they ideas, people, natural or created, what we imagine or give substance to, all will be regarded as a parent would regard such resources for the family.

+Politics will become a 'blessing,' not a right. It will be viewed as a temporary career move, not a career. Politicians will not be granted any greater entitlements than any citizen receives. No lifetime entitlements. It is meant to be about service, not getting.

+The 'environment,' of all kinds, will be prioritized. Starting with our use of & impact upon the earth. **In this, The True Family Values will guide & inspire humanity to a new vision of itself.**

From this seed idea/paradigm for relationships, the nature of power, the nature of leadership & authority, will necessarily be not only challenged, but changed. Whether one is part of government, a supervisor, an owner, a boss or parent, even if one is the police or military or even a politician or religious leaders, the ethics will be the same. One heart, always seeking to defend & manage for the greater good. Remembering...

The word 'family' applies to whom we not only assert to care for... but to whom we offer such substantial effort that beloved community is the fruit we co-create with others.

Thus? There is no limit to how much 'family' we may have...

How will I view you? How will I engage you? What legacy will define my path through life with you?
Will YOU celebrate our relationship?

Conclusion: Peace begins with me... as I act with & honor 'you', even as my enemy

"How long can you continue to offer with a heart of love? This is what determines whether you have victory or defeat." Rev Sun Myung Moon

"If you do not perceive the sincerity within yourself & yet try to move forth, each movement will miss the mark." Chuang Tzu 23, Taoism

"All interpretation of meaning, like all scientific observation, strives for clarity & verifiable accuracy of insight & comprehension. The basis for certainty in understanding can either be rational, which can be further subdivided into logical & mathematical, or it can be of an emotionally empathic & artistically appreciative quality... The highest degree of rational understanding is attained in cases involving the meanings of logically or mathematically related propositions; their meaning may be immediately & unambiguously intelligible." Max Weber

"The attitude & ethos that distinguish the politics of a civil society is civility, i.e., a solicitude for the interest of the whole society, a concern for the common good. The civil person, when he has to decide & act in a situation in which there is conflict, thinks primarily of the civil society as the object of obligations, not of the members of his family, or his village, or his party, or his ethnic group, or his social class, or his occupation." Edward Schils

"Taken objectively, morality is in itself practical, for it is the totality of the unconditionally binding laws according to which we *ought* to act, & once one has acknowledged the authority of its concept of duty, it would be utterly absurd to continue wanting to say one *cannot* do his duty." Emmanuel Kant

"God grant we will be so maladjusted that that we will be able to go out & change our world & our civilization." Rev. Martin Luther King, Jr.

"God's messenger said... "Do you know what most commonly brings people into hell? It is the two hollow things: the mouth & the private parts." Islam

"There is no greater love than a man lay down his life for another." Jesus

There was a very significant personal moment for Rev. Moon the 1st time as he prepared to visit North Korea & Kim il Sung together. His challenge?

Himself.

Moon's love of his homeland is beyond the understanding of most people, rationally, emotionally & spiritually/psychologically. His equal love of America, even as he struggled to love such unloving people, who imagined themselves as 'Christian,' was beyond most people to grasp either.

Even when imprisoned unjustly, Moon's devotion to the potential of America to serve the world in such fashion as to effect positive change never wavered or withered.

Yet, in Kim stood everything he had lost, personally, publicly & politically. The division of Korea into North & South struck him both personally & as he understood God's position & heart would be. Moon ONLY imagined a reunited people, parent to child, neighbor to neighbor.

Kim's continual dictatorship does not allow for Kim to imagine any reconciliation except a capitulation of the South to the North. For the sake of the world, for the sake of the people themselves, of the region & for freedom itself as a personal, public & political commodity, Moon sought to offer a means towards normalization of interpersonal relationships, as Koreans & as sibling family members. Yet, in spite of best efforts & investments, the sustained threat of North Korea's potential for mischief & mayhem was & is unparalleled.

For Moon, Kim &, the re-unification of the north & south was not just a personal concern, as a Korean, or as a matter of regional security, but also imagined for its significance to become a bridge to China & peace in the region. In this regard Moon's concerns were multiple & whole purpose. This does not even address the concern Moon had for the people of North Korea who have suffered such terrible deprivation on every human measurable scale.

Kim makes the term 'despot' seem like flattery.

Hence, in an amazing testimony of Moon's preparation to visit Kim, Moon admitted that this particular enemy would be most challenging to embrace sincerely, the ONLY WAY THAT MATTERED... TO BOTH MEN.

Moon spent several days in Hawaii, praying, seeking God's heart that Moon, too, would truly come to love this man; a man who was an enemy on so many levels, personal, political & religious-spiritually. Yet, in the truest sense imaginable, they are kin... In a way ONLY Koreans feel for one another.

Thus, when Moon finally engaged Kim, he could do so sincerely, this naturally affecting the undercurrent of intimate communication they naturally would share. This was critical to the success of the two men, so as to reach a place beyond the politics of the region, but where each could share in their desire for the nation they shared, sundered now for over 40 years.

It was observed & later affirmed by Moon that he felt they reached a more profound place where the future of Korea, as a unified entity, could be imagined. Where two siblings could be reconciled & restored to true family.

Recognizing the effort requiring a process, a period of time & corresponding investment. North Korea, because of its strategic placement regionally & its political & personality/ideological structure, offers China another access point west. Hence, a buffer between China & the west but a perfect foil for an ally.

With Kim's irrational, yet rational fears of the world, his adventurism into nuclear strike capabilities also strikes a major concern for more than just the region.

Moon's desire for developing relationship was proper. Kim would ONLY relinquish control of his people, that they might advance materially & in terms of personal freedom, as it served him & HIS interests. Moon's desire was to offer the security of outside investors, but of a quality as to build up North Korea, but not for it merely to become an industrial outlet for the west.

Moon sought that Kim understand that true & lasting prosperity was the result of the principles & motives guiding all effort, short or long term. But principles of mutuality & co-creation & community.

Moon knew that ONLY true principles of interpersonal relationship could both create the social environment Moon seeks for all humanity, but are also the ONLY means for engaging others. Especially one's enemy.

Moon thus allowed himself the ONLY RIGHTEOUS form of rebellion towards Kim & his politics that a truly loving person can engage. One that seeks the freedom of the slave owner, from their own 'sin.'

Thus, Moon invested in his enemy, not for profit, though many would try to assert that as part of the motive. Moon rather recognized his 'evil' brother, but embraced him as a brother, as family. He denied nothing, allowed everything its place. His concern for Kim himself thus part of the equation of engagement & ultimately, integration.

Moon has offered his whole life to the enterprise that the human being was created & natured & nurtured to participate in morally significant sustainable relationships.

There is no other purpose for which life itself offers witness.

Moon offers the ONLY example of the broadest & most significant moral integration & investment that freedom encourages from us. When freedom is used for purposes of seeking wisdom & co-creation & community.

Moon's whole life, as was Jesus' three years of public ministry, was a witness to one truth. The human value & need for a particular quality of personal & interpersonal values to impact humanity, from motive to deliverance of behaviors. Moon, as Jesus did, thus offered that freedom was ONLY meaningful to them as they could offer humanity the ONLY quality of aid to not just offer hope, but substance.

The singularity of that purpose, so self-defined & lived, either speaks to madness or a quality of both commitment & care unparalleled.

Moon, as did Jesus, gave 100% to that public effort.

We must then ask, out of a sensed need to offer an earned respect, did they hold ANYTHING back for themselves? If we measure the heart such offering takes, we are either humbled or we turn our heads in shame. Or we are so dull, we do not even understand the monument to care such commitment argues is real, as a sustained state.

Yet, neither Jesus nor Moon asks us to make THAT degree of commitment, but rather such commitment that WE walk as giants in OUR own world.

Moon & Jesus offered to the world, on behalf of a 'parent' that seeks their children through the wilderness. A parent with no hands to hold one, no arms to embrace one, no voice to comfort.

Moon & Jesus offered that to God, the parent, on behalf of their siblings. Offered to be that voice to comfort,

213

that hand up, that embrace that offers that shame only lasts as long as moral inactivity is our focus of heart. As we stand up, we reveal to ourselves what is truly then important to us, guided by the ones who will know, from personal experience. Sharing as any truly loving elder sibling would do, for the sake of all.

In this, Jesus & Moon merely ask us to assume to give freedom such a value in our own lives, by offering the patriotism that defends all humanity. A humanity needing such a quality of sustained interpersonal relationships as to require we seek such wisdom as to insure that as more than hope.

We will encounter many 'Kim's'. We may too often BE Kim.

Either way, human need, wisdom & potential offers us freedom & opportunity. The freedom to be truly human, in our being with all others, enemy or no.

The True Family Values are the keys to a citizenship in heaven… starting here. Now.

A lasting thought...

There is no doubt, 2000 years ago the Jewish people, representing the interest of all humanity, could not understand the final connecting message of a true prophet. In doing so, the legacy, life & social significance of this light unto humanity, was snuffed out, & the hope of his message was then inherited by a disparate group of individuals. But it would be covered & hidden... by false teachings.

The consequence of this inheritance, this message of Jesus, as the concluding statement of God as to the original will for humanity, now made manifest in the flesh of a true child that God could fully relate to, was now delayed in its full potential to enter the human stream as a matter of morally significant social civil experience & hence, encouraged social/civil evolution.

Jesus' generation could have ended their years in a celebration that would still be producing fruit. Jewish history still stands as the perfect example of the process & principles

EVERY parent naturally employs in the role as a parent.

This generation has made the same error... 'Jesus' again forced to accept scribes & 'Pharisees' with our secular idea of faith... rather than 'children of God,' sharing true love as the living witness to our faith; rather now our faith is the echo of silence, a silence that offers no solace for the reality it hides from our minds, but not our hearts.

"Now I say that man, & in general every rational being, exists as an end in himself & not merely as a means to be arbitrarily used by this or that will. He must in all his actions, whether directed to himself or to other rational beings, always be regarded at the same as an end... rational beings are called persons inasmuch as their nature already mark them out as ends in themselves... Such an end is one for which there can be substituted no other end to which such beings should serve merely as a means, for otherwise nothing of absolute value would be found anywhere... The practical imperative will therefore be the following" Act in such a way that your treat humanity, whether in your own person or in the person of another, always at the same time as an end & never simply as a means." Immanuel Kant

In conclusion, as God offered humanity over the millennia, one love breaches all hurdles…

Forgiveness is the love I offer my enemy because I have reached the conclusion that life, and therefore love, cannot be fulfilled without my enemy at my table & at my side, but not as my enemy.

"What is holy? These are holy; you go to bed when you want to sleep, you eat when you want to eat, & you play when you want to play." Rev. Sun Myung Moon

"I believe that unarmed truth & unconditional love will have the final word in reality." Rev. Martin Luther King, Jr

"Ever since the fall of humanity away from its destiny, Heavenly Parent sought those who could bear the shame that forgiveness exposes, so that Heavenly Parent could then offer the tools needed to reverse & restore human history. This was the search for a 'true heart'. The Last Spiritual Samurai

"Good books are the 'footnotes' of the flow of consciousness we call individuality, when confronted by the challenges, paradoxes & pure beauty of life..." The 'mad' spiritual samurai